Contents

openings—headers—corner studs—dormers—stairways—fire and draft stops—chimney and fireplace construction—summary—review questions

CHAPTER 1

Laying Out

The term *laying out* here means the process of locating and fixing reference lines which define the position of the foundation and outside walls of a building to be erected.

SELECTION OF SITE

Preliminary to laying out (sometimes called *staking out*) it is important that the exact location of the building on the lot be properly selected. In this examination, it may be wise to dig a number of small deep holes at various points, extending to a depth a little below the bottom of the basement.

The *ground water,* which is sometimes present near the surface of the earth, will (if the holes extend down to its level) appear in the bottom of the holes. This water nearly always stands at the same level in all the holes.

If possible in selecting the site for the house, it should be located so that the bottom of the basement is above the level of the ground water. This may mean locating the building at some elevated part of the lot, or reducing the depth of excavation. The availability of storm and sanitary sewers, and their depth, should have been previously investigated. The distance of the building from the curb is usually stipulated in city building ordinances.

STAKING OUT

After the approximate location has been selected, the next step is to *lay out the building lines.* The position of all corners of the building must be marked in some way so that when the excavation is begun, the workmen may know the exact boundaries of the basement walls. There are several methods of laying out these lines:

1. With layout square.
2. With surveyor's instrument.
3. By method of diagonals.

The first method will do for small jobs, but the efficient carpenter or contractor will be equipped with a level or transit, with which the lines may be laid out with precision and more convenience than by the first method.

The Lines

There are several lines which must be located at some time during construction, and they should be carefully distinguished. They are:

1. The *line of excavation,* which is the outside line.
2. The *face line* of the basement wall inside the excavation line, and in the case of masonry building.
3. The *ashlar line,* which indicates the outside of the brick or stone walls.

In the case of a wooden structure, only the two outside lines need to be located, and often only the line of the excavation is determined at the outset.

Laying Out With Layout Square

Start the layout from any point on the ground at which it is desired to place one corner of the building. By driving a stake at this point far enough to be outside the excavation line (about 3 ft.), erect a batter board as shown in Fig. 1. The batter boards *must be leveled, and must be at the same elevation.*

Suppose that the building is of rectangular shape and that the front of the building is to be parallel with the street. Starting

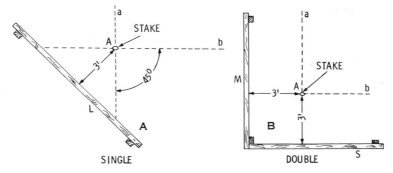

Fig. 1. Single and double batter boards. After locating a corner of the proposed building, drive down stake A and erect either a single batter board as shown in Fig. 1A or a double batter board as shown in Fig. 1B. Note the general direction of the building lines Aa and Ab, and locate the single board L, or double board MS 3 feet back from the stake.

at the stake *A*, Fig. 1 (using the double batter board) lay out a line parallel with the street as in Fig. 2. Drive a stake *B*, at a distance equal to the length of the front of the building. The exact location of the ends of the line may be indicated by a nail driven into each stake. Since the building is of rectangular shape, lines must be laid out at *A* and *B* at 90° or right angles to the line *AB*.

The right angle is obtained by means of a large square constructed as in Fig. 3. The figure shows the right way to make the square by having boards *A* and *B* the same length. It must be evident that if *A* and *B* is cut off where they are joined to *C*, making *B* shorter than *A*, the extra length of *A* does not add to the precision, as the latter depends upon the length of the shortest side. This square is shown in Fig. 4 at corner *A*.

In using the square, the legs and lines are brought into alignment by means of a plumb bob. Having placed one leg under line *AB*, adjust line *AD* on the batter boards until it is directly over the nail in stake *A*, and the other leg of the square. When the four lines *AB*, *BC*, *CD*, and *DA*, are located and the work checked by measuring diagonals *AC* and *BD* (which must be equal), the lines are located permanently by placing them in vertical slits sawed in the batter boards. Stakes *B*, *C*, and *D* may now be driven at

11

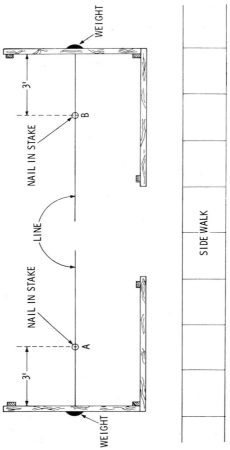

Fig. 2. Locating the front of the building. Points A and B are two stakes with nails driven in each. The distance between these two nails is the length of the front side of the building.

the corners, using a plumb bob to locate the intersections of the lines on the ground. Fig. 5 shows the use of the plumb bob, and Fig. 6 shows the method of permanently locating lines by sawing slits in the batter boards (slits *L* and *M*) for line *AD* and *AB*.

After permanently locating the four building lines, mark off on the batter boards the distance the excavation lines are from the

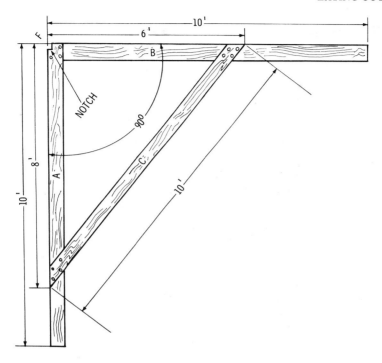

Fig. 3. To make a large layout square, use 1 X 6 boards (A, B, and C, 10 feet long) and square off ends of A, and B with precision. Mark off with care 8 feet on board A, 6 feet on board B, and 10 feet on board C. Place board A on top of board B, and Board C on top of both A and B, and fasten with nails. If this work is done with precision, an accurate right angle will be obtained at point F. The square should be notched at point F, to permit it to rest under the layout lines.

building lines, and cut slits at these points, as in Fig. 6. In excavating, the lines are placed in the outer or excavation slits, and may be later moved into the other slits as the work progresses. These lines are held taut by means of weights, as shown.

Laying Out With Transit Instruments

A transit may be used, and as this is an instrument of precision, the work of laying out is more accurate than when the layout

13

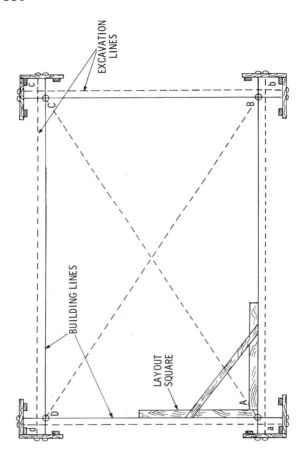

EXCAVATION LINES

BUILDING LINES

LAYOUT SQUARE

Fig. 4. Layout for a building using batter boards.

square is employed. In Fig. 7, let *ABCD* be a building already erected, and at a distance from this (at right angle) building *GHJK* will be erected. Level up the instrument at point *E,* making *A* and *E* the distance the new building will be from points *A* and *B*. Make points *B* and *F* the same length as points *A* and *E*. At this point, drive a stake in the ground at point G, making points *F* and *G* the required distance between the two buildings. Point *H*

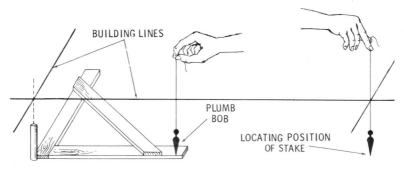

Fig. 5. Method of bringing lines and layout square into alignment, and location of points for corner stakes by means of a plumb bob.

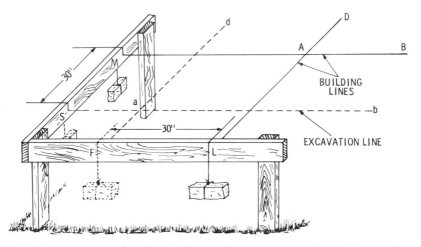

Fig. 6. Permanent location of layout lines are made by cutting in the batter board. Slits L and M locate the building lines. Approximately 30 inches away are lines F and S which are excavation lines.

will be on the same line as point *G*, making the distance between the two points as required.

Place the transit over point *G*, and level it up. Focus the transit telescope on point *E* or *F* and lock into position. Turn the horizontal circle on the transit until one of the zeros exactly coincides with the vernier zero. Loosen the clamp screw and turn the telescope and vernier 90 degrees. This will locate point *K*, which will be at

15

the desired distance from point *G*. For detailed operation of the transit, see the manufacturer's information. The level may be used in setting floor timbers, in aligning shafting, and locating drains.

Method of Diagonals

All that is needed in this method is a line, stakes, and a steel tape measure. Here, the right angle between the lines at the corners of a rectangular building is found by calculating the length of the diagonal which forms the hypotenuse of a right-angle triangle. By applying the following rule, the length of the diagonal (hypotenuse) is found.

Rule—The length of the hypotenuse of a right-angle triangle is equal to the square root of the sum of the squares of each leg.

Thus, in a right-angle triangle *ABC*, of which *AC* is the hypotenuse,

$$AC = \sqrt{AB^2 + BC^2} \quad\text{..(1)}$$

Suppose, in Fig. 9, *ABCD* represents the sides of a building to be constructed, and it is required to lay out these lines to the

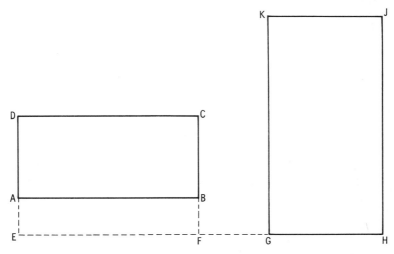

Fig. 7. Diagram illustrating method of laying out with transit instrument.

Fig. 8. A Berger builders transit, used by builders, contractors and agricultural planners for setting grades, batter boards, and various earth excavations.

dimensions given. Substitute the values given in equation (1), thus,

$$AC = \sqrt{30^2 + 40^2} = \sqrt{900 + 1600} = \sqrt{2500} = 50$$

To lay out the rectangle of Fig. 9, first locate the 40-ft. line *AB* with stake pins. Attach the line for the second side to *B,* and measure off on this line the distance *BC* (30 feet), point *C* being indicated by a knot. This distance must be accurately measured with the line at the *same tension* as in *A* and *B.*

With end of a steel tape fastened to stake pin *A,* adjust the position of the tape and line *BC* until the 50-foot division on the tape coincides with point *C* on the line. *ABC* will then be a right angle and point *C* will be properly located.

The lines for the other two sides of the rectangle are laid out in a similar manner. After thus obtaining the positions for the corner stake pins, erect the batter boards and permanent lines as

17

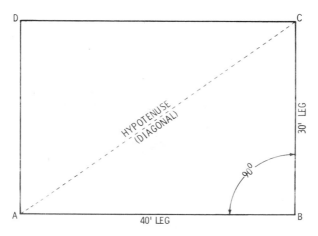

Fig. 9. *Diagram illustrating how to find the length of the diagonal in laying out lines of a rectangular building by the method of diagonals.*

shown in Fig. 6. A simple procedure may be used in laying out the foundations for a small rectangular building. Be sure that the opposite sides are equal, and then measure *both* diagonals. No matter what this distance may be, they will be equal if the building is square. No calculations are necessary, and the method is precise.

POINTS ON LAYING OUT

For ordinary residence work, a surveyor or the city engineer is employed to locate the lot lines. Once these lines are established, the builder is able to locate the building lines by measurement.

A properly prepared set of plans will show both the present contour of the ground upon which the building is to be erected, and the new grade line which is to be established after the building is completed. The most convenient method of determining old grade lines and of establishing new ones is by means of a transit, or with a Y level and a rod. Both instruments work on the same principle in grade work. As a rule, a masonry contractor has his own Y level and uses it freely as the wall is constructed, especially where levels are to be maintained as the courses of material are placed.

In locating the earth grade about a building, stakes are driven

18

into the ground at frequent intervals and the amount of "fill" indicated by the heights of these stakes. Grade levels are usually established after the builders have finished, except that the mason will have the grade indicated for him where the wall above the grade is to be finished differently than below grade. When a Ý level is not available, a 12- or 14-ft. straight edge and a common carpenter's level may be used, with stakes being driven to define the level.

SUMMARY

The term "laying out" means the process of locating a fixed reference line which will indicate the position of the foundation and walls of a building to be erected.

A problem sometimes encountered is ground water. It is sometimes present near the surface of the earth and will appear in the bottom of small deep test holes, generally at the same level. A house, should, if possible, be located so that the bottom of the basement floor is above the level of the ground water.

After the location of the house has been selected, the next step is to lay out or stake out the building lines. The position of all corners of the house must be marked so that workmen will know the exact boundaries of the basement walls.

There are several methods used in laying out a building site. Three of these methods are: with a layout square, with a surveyor's instrument, and with diagonal measurements. When laying out a site, there are several lines which must be located at some time during construction. These lines are the line of excavation, which is the outside line; the face line of the basement wall inside the excavation line; and in the case of a masonry building, the ashlar line, which indicates the outside of the brick or stone wall.

REVIEW QUESTIONS

1. What is ground water?
2. Name the three methods used in laying out a building site.
3. What is the difference between laying out and staking out?
4. What is the line of excavation?
5. What is the ashlar line?

CHAPTER 2

Foundations

The foundation is the part of a building that receives the load of the superstructure. As generally understood, the term foundation includes all walls, piers, columns, pilasters or other supports below the first floor framing.

There are two general forms of foundation; spread foundations, and pile foundations. Fig. 1. Spread foundations are the most popular type used. They receive the weight of the superstructure and distribute the weight to a stable soil base by means of individual footings. Pile foundations, on the other hand, transmit the weight of the superstructure through a weak soil to a more stable base.

There are three basic types of spread foundations; the slab-on-grade, the crawl space, and the basement, as shown in Fig. 2. Each one of the foundation systems is popular in certain geographic areas. The slab-on-grade is popular in the south and southwest; the crawl space is popular throughout the nation; and the basement is the most popular in the northern states.

SLAB-ON-GRADE

There are three basic types of slab-on-grade. The most popular type is where the footing and slab are combined to form one integral unit. Another type has the slab supported by the foundation wall and there is a type where the slab is independent of the footing and foundation wall. Fig. 3.

The procedure for constructing a slab-on-grade would be:

1. *Clear the site.* In most cases no excavation is needed, but

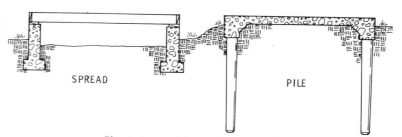

Fig. 1. General forms for foundations.

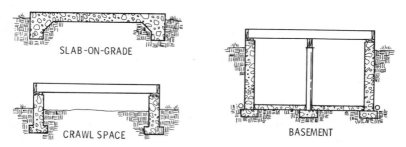

Fig. 2. Three types of spread foundations.

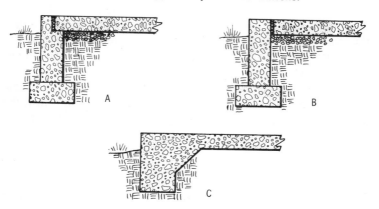

Fig. 3. Three types of slab-on-grade foundations.

some fill dirt may be needed. A tractor or dozer is usually used to remove the necessary brush and trees. It can also be used to spread the necessary fill.

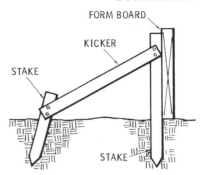

Fig. 4. Form construction.

2. *Layout the foundation.* This is usually done with batter board and strings. When the batter boards are attached to the stakes, the lowest batter board should be 8 inches above grade.

3. *Place and brace the form boards.* The form boards are usually 2 × 12's, 2 × 6's or 2 × 4's, and are aligned with the builders string. To keep the forms in proper position they are braced with 2 × 4's. One 2 × 4 is placed adjacent to the form board and another is driven at an angle three feet from the form board. Between the two 2 × 4's a "kicker" is placed to tie the two together. These braces are placed around the perimeter of the building, 4 feet on center, Fig. 4.

4. *Additional fill is brought in.* The fill should be free of debris or organic matter and should be screeded to within 8 inches of the top of the forms. The fill should then be well tamped.

5. *Footings are dug.* The footings should be a minimum of 12 inches wide and should extend 6 inches into undisturbed soil. The footings should also extend one foot below the frost line.

6. *Place the base course.* The base course is usually wash gravel or crushed stone and is placed 4 inches thick. The base course acts as a capillary stop for any moisture that might rise through the soil.

7. *Place the vapor barrier.* The vapor barrier is a sheet of .006 polyethylene and acts as a secondary barrier against moisture penetration.

23

8. *Reinforce the slab.* In most cases, the slab is reinforced with 6 × 6 No. 10 gauge wire mesh. To insure that the wire mesh is properly embedded, metal chairs are used to elevate the wire.

9. *Reinforce the footings.* The footings are usually reinforced with three or four deformed metal bars 18 to 20 feet in length. The rods should not terminate at a corner, but should be bent to project around it. At an intersection of two rods, there should be an 18 inch overlap.

Once the forms are set and the slab bed completed, concrete is brought in and placed in position. The concrete should be placed in small piles and as near to its final location as possible. Small areas of concrete should be worked—in working large areas the water will supersede the concrete, causing inferior concrete. Once the concrete has been placed in the forms, it should be worked around the reinforcing bars and into the corners of the forms. If the concrete is not properly "worked" air pockets or honeycombs might appear.

Fig. 5. Hand tamping or "jitterbugging" concrete to place large aggregate below the surface. The other man (bent over) is screeding with a long 2×4 to proper grade.

Fig. 6. The darby being used after the jitterbug process.

After the concrete has been placed, it must be struck or screeded to the proper grade. A long straight edge is usually used in the process. It is moved back and fourth in a saw like motion until the concrete is level with the forms. To place the large aggregate below the surface, the concrete is hand tamped or "jitterbugged." Fig. 5. A darby is used immediately after the jitterbug and is also used to embed the large aggregate. Fig. 6. To produce a "round" on the edge of the concrete slab, an edger is used. The "round" keeps the concrete from chipping off and it increases the aesthetic appeal of the slab. Fig. 7. After the water sheen has left the surface of the slab, it is floated. Floating is used to remove imperfections and to compact the surface of the concrete. For a smooth and dense surface the concrete is then troweled. It can be trowled with a steel hand trowel or it can be troweled with a power trowel. Fig. 8.

Once the concrete has been finished, it should be cured. There are three ways that the slab might be cured: (1) burlap coverings, (2) sprinkling, (3) and ponding. Regardless of the technique used, the slab should be kept moist at all times.

25

Fig. 7. Using an edger to round off the edges.

Fig. 8. Using a power trowel.

A CRAWL SPACE

A crawl space foundation system can be constructed of an independent footing and concrete block foundation wall, or the footing and foundation wall can be constructed of concrete.

The footing should be constructed of concrete and should be placed below the frost line. The projection of the footing pass the foundation wall should equal ½ the thickness of the foundation wall. Fig. 9. The thickness of the footing should equal the width of the foundation wall. There are two basic ways to form a footing for a crawl space. One of the most popular ways is to dig a footing trench and place the concrete in the trench. To maintain the proper elevation grade stakes are placed in the trench. The other technique is to use form boards. If form boards are used they should be properly erected and braced. In some cases, additional strength may be needed, so to alleviate some of the weaknesses of plain concrete, reinforcement is added.

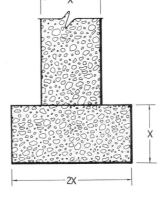

Fig. 9. Illustrating the footing construction.

Most of the concrete used in the footings is mixed in a batch plant and delivered to the job site in a truck. But, if the concrete is to be mixed at the job site it should have 6 gallons of water to a sack of cement, when using average wet sand. The water shall be free from impurities; that is, it shall be fit to drink. Concrete for footings shall be machine mixed (if possible) and shall be in the approximate proportions of 1 volume of cement to 2¾ volume of sand and 4 volumes of gravel or crushed stone. The proportion of sand and gravel may be varied slightly as long as the mix is workable and plastic, but the amount of water per sack of cement should not be changed. Forms are removed after the concrete has hardened. Before laying the concrete masonry, the top of the footings should be swept clean of dirt or loose material.

Regardless of whether the foundation wall is constructed of placed concrete, or concrete blocks, the top should be a minimum of 18 inches above grade. This allows for proper ventilation, repair work, and visual inspection.

BASEMENT CONSTRUCTION

The foundation wall, in basement construction, should be built with the utmost care and craftsmanship, for in many cases ground water erodes the soil from beneath the foundation and seeps into the basement. Fig. 10.

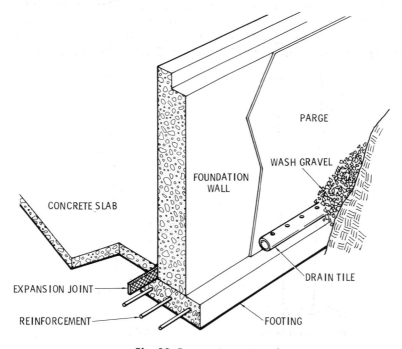

Fig. 10. Basement construction.

To properly dampproof the basement wall, a 4 inch drain tile should be placed at the base of the foundation wall. The drain tile can be laid with open joints or it can have small openings along the top. The tile should be placed in a bed of wash gravel or crushed stone and should drain into a dry stream bed or storm sewer. The foundation wall should then be parged with masonry cement, mopped with hot asphalt, or covered with polyethylene. These techniques will keep moisture from seeping through the foundation wall. For further protection, all surface water should be directed away from the foundation system. This can be achieved by discharging the water through a downspout and sloping the finished grade away from the house.

PILE FOUNDATION

Pile foundations are used to minimize and reduce settlement. There are two classifications of piles; point bearing and friction. Fig. 11. Point bearing piles transmit loads through weak soil to an area that has a better bearing surface. The friction pile depends

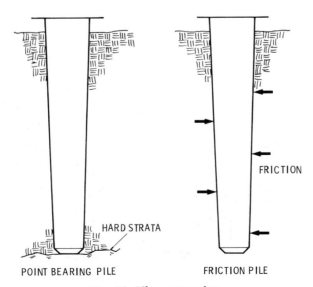

FRICTION

HARD STRATA

POINT BEARING PILE   FRICTION PILE

Fig. 11. Pile construction.

on the friction between the soil and the pile to support the imposed load.

Many different types of materials are used for piles, but the most common are concrete, timber and steel.

SUMMARY

There are two general forms of foundations: spread foundations and pile foundations. Spread foundations are the most popular type used. There are three basic types of spread foundations: the slab-on-grade; the crawl space, and the basement.

The procedure for constructing a slab-on-grade would be: clear the site, layout the foundation, place and brace the form boards, add fill, dig the footings, place the base course, place the vapor barrier, reinforce the slab, and reinforce the footings.

The foundation wall, in basement construction, should be built with the utmost care and craftsmanship, for in many cases ground water erodes the soil from beneath the foundation and seeps into the basement.

REVIEW QUESTIONS

1. What are the two general forms of foundations?
2. What is a foundation?
3. Why is base course used?
4. How is a concrete slab cured?
5. How is a basement wall damproofed?

CHAPTER 3

Concrete Forms

Since a concrete mixture is semi-fluid, it will take the shape of anything into which it is poured. Moulds or *forms* are necessary to hold the concrete to the required shape until it hardens. Such forms or moulds are almost invariably made of metal, sheet steel, or wood.

The length of time necessary to leave the forms in place depends on the nature of the structure. For small construction work where the concrete bears external weight, the forms may be removed as soon as the concrete will bear its own weight, which is between 12 and 48 hours after the concrete has been poured. Where the concrete must resist the pressure of the earth or water (as in retaining walls or dams), the forms should be left in place until the concrete has developed to its final strength; this may be as long as three or four weeks.

Forms must be reasonably tight, rigid and strong enough to sustain the weight of the concrete. They should also be simple and economical and designed so that they may be easily removed and re-erected without damage to themselves or to the concrete. The different shapes into which the concrete is formed means that each job will present some new problems to be solved.

LUMBER FOR FORMS

Most concrete building construction is done by using wooden or plywood forms. If kiln dried lumber is used it should be thoroughly wet before concrete is placed. This is because the lumber will absorb water from the concrete, and if the forms are made tight (as they should be), the swelling from absorption will cause the forms to buckle or warp. Oiling or greasing the inside of forms before use is recommended, especially where forms are to be used repeatedly. It prevents absorption of water, assists in keeping them in shape when not in use, and makes their removal from around the concrete much easier.

Spruce or pine seems to be the best all around material. It can be obtained in almost any location, and is undoubtedly an excellent lumber to use for joist, studs, and posts. For sheathing, white pine is better because of its smoothness and resistance to warping. Hemlock is not usually desirable, especially for concrete form work. This wood is too coarse grained to be suitable for sheathing, and is liable to warp when exposed to the weather or concrete.

Form lumber should be free from loose knots or other defects and irregularities that would be reproduced by the concrete. It is often possible to build forms from stock lengths of lumber, without cutting, thereby saving material and labor. It is seldom economical to rework secondhand lumber for forms.

PREPARATION OF THE LUMBER

All lumber should be dressed at least on one side and both edges, and in most cases it will be cheaper to have it dressed on both sides. Dressing is necessary in order to keep the face next to the concrete uniform. In footings and rough work that is not to show, practically any lumber can be used that will hold wet concrete.

In face work, where a smooth and true surface is important, the lumber employed should be dressed on all four sides. The edges may be cut square, mitered, or tongue and groove. For fine finished work, the inside of the board forms are sometimes covered with oiled hardboard. Contrary to opinion, hardboard-lined forms may be used time after time. Plywood forms will often show the grain in the wood.

A beveled edge joint is desirable where dry lumber is used, because buckling is prevented by the edges crushing as the boards swell. The tongue and groove joint, however, gives the best results under ordinary conditions. The tongue and groove joint is more expensive than the beveled edge joint, but it gives smoother surfaces after repeated use. Joints in forms for columns, beams, and girders are sometimes made tight simply by dressing the lumber true to edge, forming a square or butt joint.

CLASSIFICATION OF FORMS

Numerous types of forms are used to meet the varied requirements. These various types may be classified
(1) With respect to the material, as:
    a. Wood.
    b. Metal.
    c. Composite.

(2) With respect to shape, as:
    a. Straight.
    b. Circular.

(3) With respect to solid or hollow casts, as:
    a. Single.
    b. Double.

(4) With respect to method of construction, as:
    a. Ordinary.
    b. Unit.

(5) With respect to part of structure used for, as:
    a. Foundation.
    b. Wall.
    c. Steps.
    d. Sidewalks, etc.

Most forms are now made of wood or plywood although steel forms are often used for work on large flat surfaces, such as sidewalks, curbs, roads, retaining walls, and columns where the forms are to be used repeatedly. The erection and removal are the chief factors in economical designs of forms, and each job should be thoroughly studied and forms designed with this point in mind.

CONSTRUCTION OF FORMS

Since concrete weighs from 130 to 150 lbs per cu. ft., forms should be of substantial construction and properly proportioned so they will be rigid against pressures due to the weight of the material, thus avoiding any bulging of vertical forms or sagging of horizontal forms. Any sagging will result in small cracks developing while the concrete is hardening, preventing the construction from having the desired strength.

To retain the concrete in position in its plastic condition and until it hardens, forms are needed and are often constructed by using the following parts:

1. Retaining boards.
2. Supporters, or studs.
3. Braces.

The ordinary arrangement of these members is shown in Fig. 1. The thickness of the lumber varies according to its use. For short spans between supports, such as floor slabs and wall forms, 1-inch thick is generally used. For columns, either 1-in. or 1¼-in. lumber is used according to the spacing of the yokes. For beam sides and bottoms, 2-inch material is used. For supports, 2 × 4, 2 × 6, or in extreme cases, 2 × 8 studs are used. The volume of the concrete and its depth determines the dimension and spacing of the supports. Forms constructed of 2 × 4 supports with 1-inch retaining boards should have studs spaced not more than two feet apart. This is to prevent bulging of the sheathing when subjected to pressure of the concrete until it hardens.

Instead of the cleat braces shown in Fig. 1, sometimes twisted tie wires with spacers are used as shown in Fig. 2. If bolts are to be used, they may be greased before the concrete is poured so they can be driven out when the forms are removed. It is best to break the bond of the concrete around such bolts within 24 hours. This may be done by merely tapping them with a hammer. Wire ties are generally used and are cut when taking down forms. All of the wire, except the projecting ends, is left in the concrete.

FOUNDATION FORMS

For small foundations, no forms are necessary if the soil is firm. In such case the trench is dug the exact size and filled with

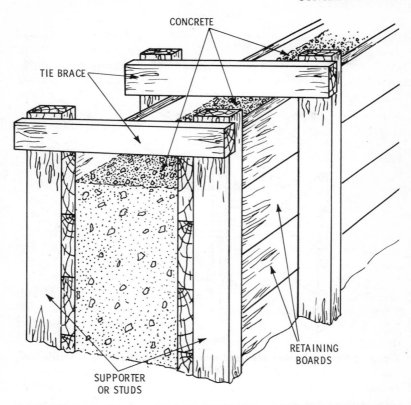

CONCRETE

TIE BRACE

RETAINING BOARDS

SUPPORTER OR STUDS

Fig. 1. Elements of a concrete form showing the principle members used, such as the retaining boards, supports, and braces.

concrete, care being taken not to knock earth from the sides into the fresh mix. With firm earth, and where an excavation is made for a small basement, a form for the inside of the foundation wall will be all that is needed. For a framed structure, sill bolts may be cast into the concrete by placing the bolts in position on top of the form as shown in Fig. 4, and pouring the concrete around them.

WALL FORMS

For walls above ground, two side forms are required. As mentioned before, these should be of substantial construction to pre-

35

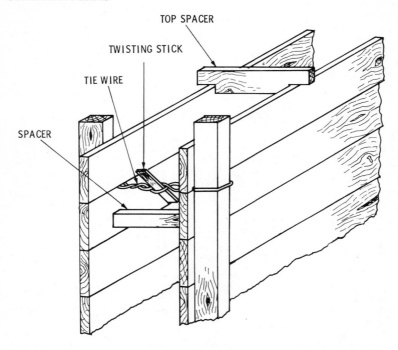

TOP SPACER

TWISTING STICK

TIE WIRE

SPACER

Fig. 2. Twisted wire ties are used with spacers to hold the concrete form together.

vent bulging by the lateral pressure due to the weight of the concrete in its plastic condition. These may be of several types, such as:

1. Continuous.
2. Full unit.
3. Lay unit (continuous or sectional).

Fig. 5 shows the details of continuous forms with side struts and through ties. The forms are braced strongly against the ground on both sides, and are self-supporting, with the through ties preventing spreading or bulging. The spacers keep the two sides of the form at the correct distance apart. To economize on lumber, the wall may be progressively built in sections, using a full unit form extending from bottom to top of the wall as in Fig. 6. This

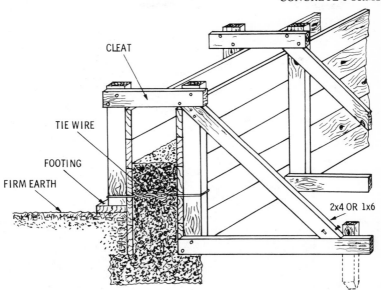

CONCRETE FORMS

CLEAT

TIE WIRE

FOOTING

FIRM EARTH

2x4 OR 1x6

Fig. 3. A single side foundation form, used for forming foundation in firm earth.

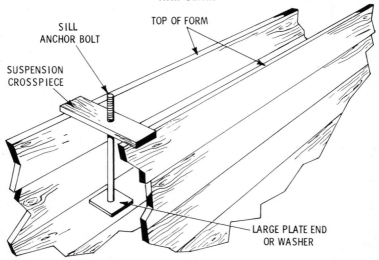

SILL
ANCHOR BOLT

TOP OF FORM

SUSPENSION
CROSSPIECE

LARGE PLATE END
OR WASHER

Fig. 4. A method of suspending a sill anchor bolt for casting in concrete.

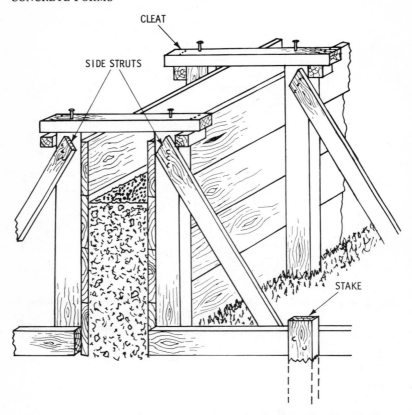

Fig. 5. Continuous wall forms with side struts and through ties.

permits a long wall to be built, the same form being used for the different sections. As soon as the first section is complete, the form is removed and placed in position for the next section, as shown in Fig. 7. The other end is closed by a vertical board with a wedge-shaped block on the inside. This makes a recess at the end of one section so that the concrete poured for the next section will make a tight joint, keying into the concrete previously poured.

Where lumber is expensive, or to reduce the amount required, the layer-unit type of form may be used as shown in Fig. 8. The form consists of two parts, an upper and lower. After pouring the lower layer of concrete into section *L* of the form, the upper section *F* is placed in position as shown. The form is held in alignmer.t by the end of the completed section *W*, and by the closed end *E*. The through braces *M* and *S* should be thoroughly greased so they can be removed easily from the concrete. The method of providing opening in walls for windows is shown in Fig. 9.

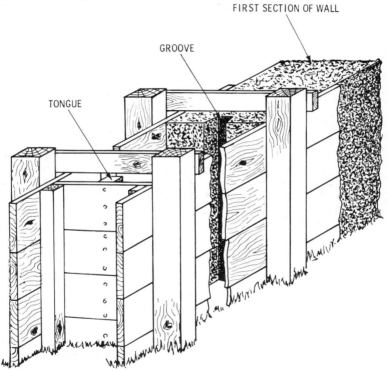

FIRST SECTION OF WALL

GROOVE

TONGUE

Fig. 6. Full unit form for casting long walls in sections. The tongue at the closed end of the forms make a good bonding groove for newly deposited concrete.

For basement walls of placed concrete, prefabricated panels are often used. Fig. 10. The panels can be made up in different widths and lengths, but the most common dimensions are 2′ × 8′. To hold the panels together a peg and wedge system is used. Fig. 11.

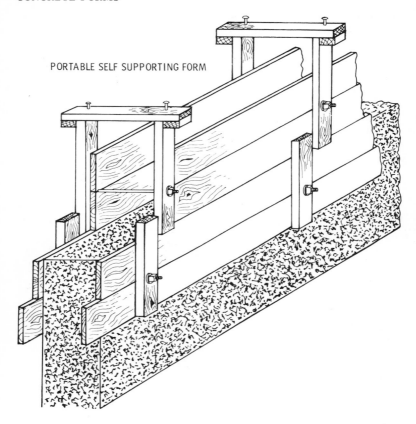

PORTABLE SELF SUPPORTING FORM

Fig. 7. A portable self supporting form, using a minimum of lumber.

FORMS FOR RECTANGULAR PIERS AND COLUMNS

These are simply boxlike forms open at the ends and suitably braced. They are of two general types:

1. Continuous.
2. Sectional.

The *continuous* form extends from the bottom to the top of the pier or column and is non-adjustable, being suitable for short piers

40

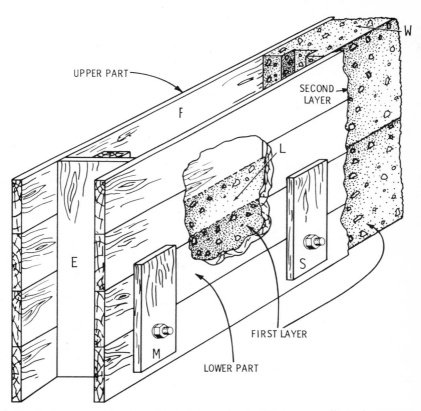

UPPER PART

SECOND LAYER

F

L

E

W

S

M

FIRST LAYER

LOWER PART

Fig. 8. Layer unit (sectional type) form for building up walls in layers.

or columns only. Such forms should be slightly tapered as shown in Fig. 12, so that they can be lifted off the concrete after it sets. *Tapered forms must be anchored down.* This is usually done by looped rods cast into the footings with attaching wires tied to a cross piece over the top of the form. The cross piece is often used for positioning anchor bolts, if any are used. Larger columns, because of the great pressure near the bottom due to the weight of the concrete, must have more substantial forms, especially if cast in one pouring.

Very heavy forms may be avoided by building up the column in several sections, using *sectional forms*. The forms are used several times for the several sections, and are held together by bolts and wedged side pieces, as shown in Fig. 13. Many types of steel column clamps are available. Most of them are tightened by means of small stay wedges. All of them are fully adjustable for different sizes of volumns.

After pouring one section, the form can usually be taken off within one to two days, and the form reset for the next section. For tapered columns, the reduction in the size of the column is obtained by removing a strip along one edge of the sides which do not have the yokes projecting and by removing a strip off one of the boards on the sides having projecting yokes. New bolt holes are either bored in the yokes, or packing strips are placed on the yokes for the wedges to bear against. If there

CORE BOX

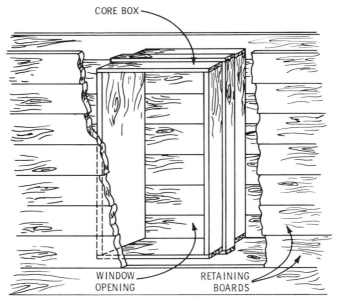

WINDOW OPENING   RETAINING BOARDS

Fig. 9. Core box placed in a wall form for window opening.

is a boring machine on the job, the yokes should have a series of holes bored in them before they are fastened to the column sides, so that it will not be necessary for the carpenters to bore them by hand.

Courtesy Symous Corp.

Fig. 10. Prefabricated build-up panels used for concrete forms.

Forms for octagonal columns are made as shown in Fig. 14. This column is identical to the one shown in Fig. 13 except that the pieces are inserted in the corners to give the column eight sides. The flare is made at the top of the column by fitting in triangular pieces of wood. Since fresh concrete is practically liquid and over twice as heavy as water, the column form must be designed to withstand the bursting pressure of the concrete. This will make it necessary to have the yokes closer together at the bottom than at the top.

In place of bolts, rods with a malleable iron clamp fastened in place with a set of screws are often used for form work. These clamps may be obtained from supply houses. The clamp is slipped over the rod and brought to a firm bearing by a device furnished by the makers of the clamps. Then the set screw in the clamp

Courtesy Symous Corp.

Fig. 11. Peg and wedge system used to connect and hold prefabricated panels together.

Another method of clamping columns is to use column clamps. These clamps are made of steel and have permanently attached wedges to pull the clamp tight. The standard size clamp is 36, 48 and 60 inches, Fig. 15.

Spacing of Yokes for Columns

The accompanying Table 1 will be found useful in proportioning columns of various sizes. The method of using the table is illustrated in the following example .

Example—To find the spacing of yokes for a 24 × 18 column 10-ft. high, use the column headed 24". Read up the column from the 10-ft. line and the spacing of the yokes will be found to be 14" for the bottom yoke, 16" for the next upper yoke, 22" for the next, and so on to the top (see Fig. 16).

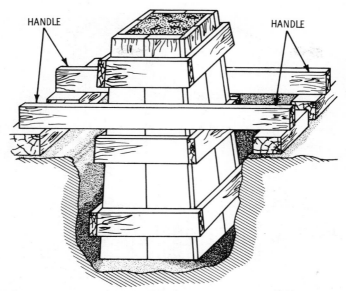

Fig. 12. Continuous form for rectangular short pier or column. The pier can be leveled by putting blocks under the handles of the form.

FORMS FOR CONCRETE ROOFS

Since concrete weighs from 130 to 150 pounds per cubic foot, floor and roof forms must be designed with a sufficient factor of safety, to prevent them from sagging from their own weight as well as that of the concrete. Any sagging of forms will result in small cracks developing while the concrete is hardening, and these will gradually widen, preventing the construction from having the desired strength. Enough braces, struts and studs must be used in the forms to prevent sagging. Forms for roofs should not be removed for at least three weeks. It is very important that roofs have plenty of time to harden before forms are removed.

CIRCULAR FORMS

Circular forms are of two types—*movable* and *stationary*. This type of form is generally laid out on a floor, or on level ground, by means of a stake at the center and the use of a compass stick

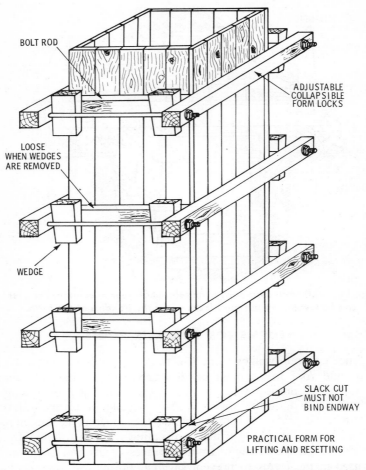

BOLT ROD

ADJUSTABLE
COLLAPSIBLE
FORM LOCKS

LOOSE
WHEN WEDGES
ARE REMOVED

WEDGE

SLACK CUT
MUST NOT
BIND ENDWAY

PRACTICAL FORM FOR
LIFTING AND RESETTING

*Fig. 13. Sectional forms for long rectangular columns, using through
bolt ties, and wedge adjustments.*

with holes at each end, the distance between being equal to the
radius of the circle. The hole at one end is used for fastening the
stick to the stake and the hole at the other end is for a pencil
to mark the circle.

In constructing tall tanks or silos, the forms are wedged in place
and filled with concrete. When the concrete is sufficiently hard

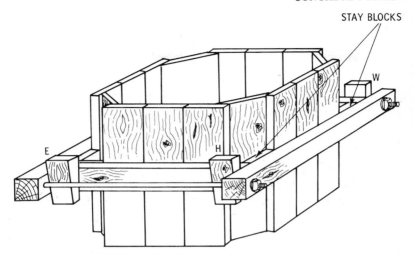

STAY BLOCKS

W

E

H

*Fig. 14. Detail of form for an octagonal column. Positions E, H and W,
are wedges.*

the wedges are loosened and the forms raised, guided by the uprights and wedged in place and again filled. Movable or slip
forms work very advantageously on certain classes of work, such
as silos and grain tanks, since they can be moved by jacks.

Steel circular column forms are also used in the construction of
concrete columns. Fig. 17. The forms are constructed of heavy
gauge steel and have all ends and edges reinforced with angles.
Most of the forms have diameters of 18, 24, 30 and 36 inches and
are available in lengths of 36, 48, 60, 72, 96, 120, and 144 inches.

DOUBLE FORMS

When a solid wall is constructed, it is a simple matter to set
up an outside and an inside form. However, to economize on
material and obtain the advantage of air-core insulation, double
or hollow-core forms are used. The demand for hollow concrete
walls has developed the double forms, some of which have been
patented.

47

Table 1. Yoke Spacing for Columns

HEIGHT IN FEET	LARGEST DIMENSION OF COLUMN IN INCHES							
	16	18	20	24	28	30	32	36
1								17
2	31	29	27	23	21	20	19	
3				23	21	20	19	17
4	31	28	26					17
5				23	20	19	18	15
6			26		18	18	17	
7	30	28		22			13	12
8			24		15	18	12	11
9	29	26		16	13	12	10	10 / 8
10			19	14	12	12	10	8 / 7
11	21	20	16	13	10	10 / 9	8	7 / 7
12		18	16	12	9 / 9	8	8	7 / 6
13	20		15	11	9 / 9	8 / 8	7 / 7	6 / 6
14		16	14	10	8	7 / 7	7 / 6	6
15	16	15	12	9 / 9	8 / 8	7 / 7	6 / 6	
16	15	13	11	9 / 9	7 / 6			
17	14	12	11	8 / 8				
18	13	12	10 / 10	8 / 8				
19	13	11	10					
20	12	11	9					

Fig. 18 shows a type of double form in closed and open (or releasing) position. Assuming that the average size of the building is 25′ × 50′, three men can pour or fill an 18-inch course and set the reinforcing bars in one day, so that the work may proceed promptly the next day. There should be no attempt made to have the walls smooth. The rough texture gives better adhesion to the finish coating which will be applied later. An 8-in. hollow wall with a 2-in. air space is one-quarter lighter and requires one-quarter less material than if poured solid; also it saves the need of

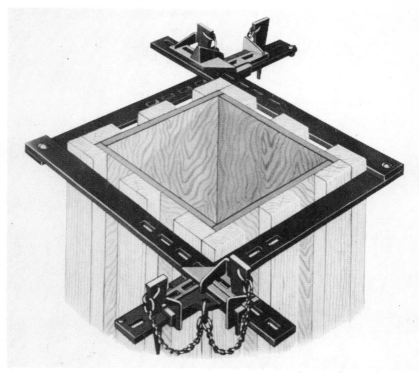

Courtesy Symous Corp.

Fig. 15. Steel column clamps.

damp proofing and furring the inside wall for plastering. Loose-fill insulation may be poured in the cavity.

POINTERS ON FORMS AND THEIR USE

Concrete will not stick to forms that are oiled each time before use with a mixture of boiled linseed oil and kerosene (equal parts of each). If not oiled, they should at least be thoroughly wetted down. They should be carefully cleaned of all particles of old concrete after removal, and be wet down immediately before using again. Forms for the ordinary types of square or rectangular watering troughs, hog feeding troughs, and manure pits, are all simple types, and when the earth is firm enough to be

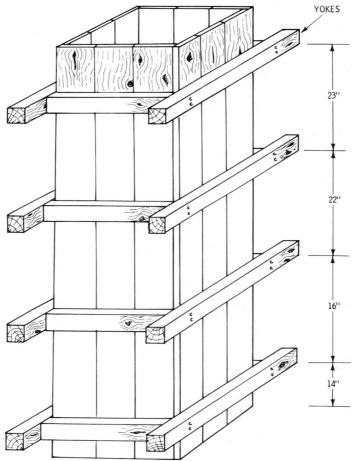

YOKES

23"

22"

16"

14"

Fig. 16. A sectional forming showing the proper yoke spacings for a 18×24 in. column 10 ft. high (see sample problem).

self-sustaining, only an inside form will be necessary. Otherwise, form construction simply amounts to one frame within another —two bottomless boxes of different sizes, one set inside the other. Forms for square or rectangular tanks that are to be built above ground should provide for a batter or slope on the inside

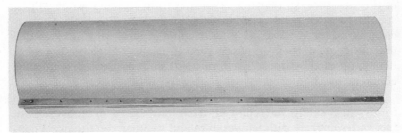

Fig. 17. Circular metal concrete form.

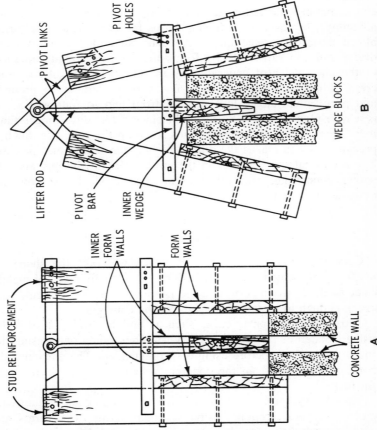

Fig. 18. A double hollow wall form. A in closed position; B in open or released position.

of the structure, so that the expansion from freezing water will be spent upward instead of against the tank sides. For tanks such as cisterns, which are usually placed underground, a form is needed for the cement roof or cover slab. This is in the nature of a floor supported by studs. The forms and studs are removed after the concrete has hardened, leaving a cover of the correct dimensions.

There is no possibility of stating with precision the time when forms may safely be removed from any piece of construction; this varies entirely with temperature and weather conditions. Whenever the structure is one which supports no weight but its own, such as a building wall of medium dimensions, above ground, forms can sometimes be removed in three or four days. There is no advantage, however, in removing forms too early, since the forms afford desirable protection to the concrete and prevent it from drying out too rapidly. The forms also prevent rapid radiation of the chemical heat generated by the curing action of the concrete. Forms for heavy arches, floors supported above ground, and roofs, must all be left in place from two to four weeks. It is a wise plan to leave the forms in place a few days longer than may seem absolutely necessary, just to be on the safe side. Such a precaution often makes the difference between failure and success. The use of calcium chloride in the mix accelerates setting, and for winter concreting, reduces the time during which the concrete must be protected.

SUMMARY

Concrete mixture is a semifluid which will take the shape of any form into which it is poured. Forms are usually made of metal, sheet steel, or wood. Forms must be reasonably tight, rigid, and strong enough to sustain the weight of the concrete.

Most concrete construction, such as building walls, is done by using wooden or plywood forms. Very often, oiling or greasing the inside of the form before using is recommended. This prevents absorption of water from the concrete which could buckle or warp the forms.

Very heavy forms may be avoided by building up columns or walls in several sections, using sectional forms. The forms are used several times for the sections, and are held together with bolts and wedged side pieces. After pouring one section, the forms can usually be taken off within one to two days, and the forms can be reset for the next section.

To economize on material and obtain the advantage of air-core insulation, double or hollow-core walls are poured. Special hollow-core forms can be constructed or purchased which usually develop an 8-inch hollow wall with a 2-inch air space. This type of wall is one-quarter lighter and requires one-quarter less concrete than a solid wall.

REVIEW QUESTIONS

1. Why is green lumber preferred for concrete forms?
2. Many times concrete forms are oiled or greased. Why is this done?
3. What are section forms?
4. Why are hollow-core walls constructed?
5. How much does concrete weigh per cubic foot?

CHAPTER 4

Concrete Block Construction

Concrete blocks provide suitable building units. By the use of standard size hollow blocks, basement walls can be erected at a very reasonable cost and are durable, light in weight, fire resistive, and able to carry heavy loads.

The term *concrete masonry* is applied to building units molded from concrete and laid by masons in a wall. The units are made of Portland cement, water, and suitable aggregates such as sand, gravel, crushed stone, cinders, burned shale, or processed slag. The various steps in building concrete masonry walls are approximately as follows:

1. Mixing the mortar.
2. Building the wall between corners.
3. Applying mortar to the blocks.
4. Placing and setting the blocks.
5. Tooling the mortar joints.
6. Building around door and window frames.
7. Placing sills and lintels.
8. Building interior walls.
9. Attaching sills and plates.

WALL THICKNESS

Thickness of concrete masonry walls is usually governed by Building Codes, if any are in existence at the particular location. Eight inches is generally specified as the minimum thickness for all exterior walls, and for load-bearing interior walls. Partitions and curtain walls are often made 3, 4, or 6 inches thick. The thickness of bearing walls in heavily loaded buildings is properly governed by the loading. Allowable working loads are commonly 70 pounds per square inch (70 p.s.i.) of gross wall area when laid in 1:1:6 (1 volume of Portland cement, 1 volume of lime putty or hydrated lime, and 6 parts damp, loose mortar sand). On small jobs, masonry cement can be purchased and the mortar mixed with 1 part masonry cement to 3 parts sand (mix dry before adding water). A mortar mix can also be obtained to which all you add is water. When a mortar of maximum strength is

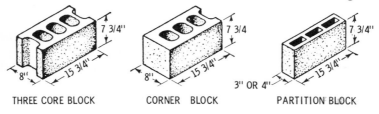

THREE CORE BLOCK   CORNER BLOCK   PARTITION BLOCK

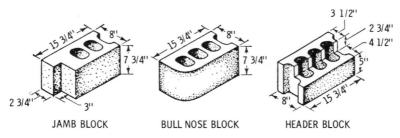

JAMB BLOCK   BULL NOSE BLOCK   HEADER BLOCK

Fig. 1. Illustrating common size and shapes of concrete masonry blocks.

desired for use in load bearing walls, or walls subjected to heavy pressure and subjected to freezing and thawing, a mortar made of 1 part Portland cement, 1 part masonry cement, and not more than 6 parts sand is recommended.

Shapes and Sizes of Standard Masonry Units

Concrete masonry units, often referred to as concrete blocks, are made in several sizes and shapes. The shapes and sizes of the

56

most generally used units are shown in Fig. 1. The 7 3/4 × 8 × 15 3/4-inch unit (usually considered 8 × 8 × 16) is the size most commonly used. The 8 × 8 × 16-inch size laid up in a single thickness produces a wall 8-inches thick with courses 8-inches in height. One course is equivalent to three brick courses.

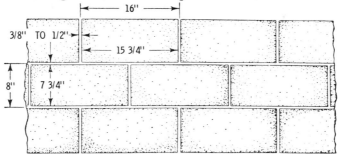

Fig. 2. Showing typical dimensions of mortar joints when using concrete blocks as building units.

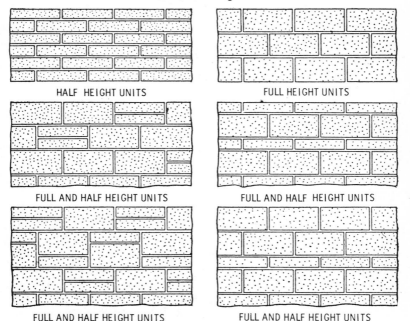

HALF HEIGHT UNITS

FULL HEIGHT UNITS

FULL AND HALF HEIGHT UNITS

FULL AND HALF HEIGHT UNITS

FULL AND HALF HEIGHT UNITS

FULL AND HALF HEIGHT UNITS

Fig. 3. Illustrating various types of patterns that can be produced with standard concrete block units.

Actual heights and lengths of the block are usually about 1/4 to 3/8-inch scant to allow for the thickness of the mortar joints, as illustrated in Fig. 2. A special corner block has one finished square end for use at the corners of the wall. A special jamb block for window and door frames is also made, as illustrated. All of the units shown are made in half lengths and quarters, as well as in full lengths, to permit breaking the vertical joints in alternate courses. Units are also made in widths of approximately 4, 6, and 12-inches.

Concrete made with sand, gravel, and crushed stone, weighs approximately 145 pounds per cubic foot. Concrete blocks made from such aggregates are known as heavyweight units. Those made with cinders, burned shale, and processed slags, weigh approximately two-thirds as much as heavyweight units, and have a greater heat insulating value. Thus, from that standpoint, it may be advisable to use lightweight units where heat comfort is a major consideration, but they do not have the strength of heavyweight units. Fig. 3 shows a number of various designs that can be obtained by using different size concrete blocks.

WALL CONSTRUCTION

Concrete masonry walls subject to average loading and exposure should be laid up with mortar composed of 1 volume of masonry cement and between 2 and 3 volumes of damp, loose mortar sand; or 1 volume of Portland cement, between 1 and 1 1/4 volumes of hydrated lime or lime putty, and between 4 and 6 volumes of damp, loose mortar sand. Enough water is added to produce a workable mixture.

Concrete masonry walls and isolated piers subject to severe conditions, such as extremely heavy loads, violent winds, earthquakes, severe frost action, or other conditions requiring extra strength, should be laid up with mortar composed of 1 volume of masonry cement, plus 1 volume of Portland cement, and between 4 and 6 volumes of damp, loose mortar sand; or 1 volume of Portland cement, between 2 and 3 volumes of damp, loose mortar sand and up to 1/4 volume of hydrated lime or lime putty. Enough water is added to produce a workable mixture.

58

Laying Blocks At Corners

In laying up corners with concrete masonry blocks, place a taut line all the way around the foundation, with the ends of the string tied together. It it customary to lay up the corner blocks three or four courses high and use them as guides in laying the walls.

A full width of mortar is placed on the footing, as shown in Fig. 4, with the first course laid 2 or 3 blocks long each way from the corner. The second course is a half block shorter each way than the first course; the third course is a half block shorter than the second, etc. Thus the corners are stepped back until only the corner blocks are laid. Use a line and level frequently to see that the block are laid straight and that the corners are plumb. It is customary that such special units as corner blocks, door- and window-jamb blocks, fillers, veneer blocks, etc., be provided prior to commencing the laying of the blocks.

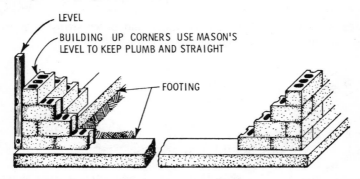

LEVEL

BUILDING UP CORNERS USE MASON'S LEVEL TO KEEP PLUMB AND STRAIGHT

FOOTING

Fig. 4. Laying up corners when building with concrete masonry block units.

Building Walls Between Corners

In laying walls between corners, a line is stretched tightly from corner to corner to serve as a guide (Fig. 5). The line is fastened to nails or wedges driven into the mortar joints so that, when stretched, it just touches the upper outer edges of the block laid in the corners. The blocks in the wall between corners are laid so that they will just touch the cord in the same manner. In this way, straight horizontal joints are secured. Prior to laying up the

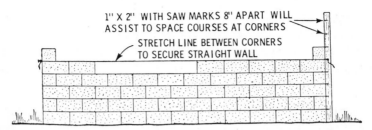

Fig. 5. Showing procedure in laying concrete block walls.

outside wall, the door and window frames should be on hand to set in place as guides for obtaining the correct opening.

Applying Mortar to Blocks

The usual practice is to place the mortar in two separate strips, both for the horizontal or bed joints and for the vertical or end joints, as shown in Fig. 6. The mortar is applied only on the face shells of the block. This is known as *face-shell bedding*. The air spaces thus formed between the inner and outer strips of mortar will help produce a dry wall.

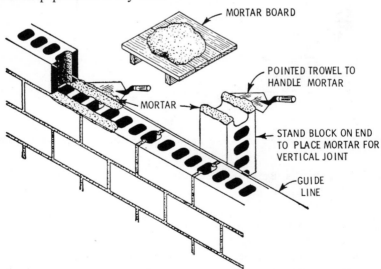

Fig. 6. The usual practice in applying mortar to concrete blocks.

Masons often stand the block on end and apply mortar for the end joint. Sufficient mortar is put on to make sure that the joint will be well filled. Some masons apply mortar on the end of the block previously laid, as well as on the end of the block to be laid next to it, to make certain that the vertical joint will be completely filled.

Placing and Setting Blocks

In placing, the block which has mortar applied to one end is then picked up, as shown in Fig. 7, and shoved firmly against the block previously placed. Note that the mortar is already in place in the bed or horizontal joints.

Mortar squeezed out of the joints is carefully cut off with the trowel and applied on the other end of the block, or thrown back onto the mortar board for use later. The blocks are laid to touch the guide line, and tapped with the trowel to get them straight and

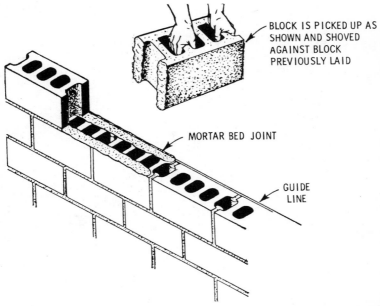

BLOCK IS PICKED UP AS SHOWN AND SHOVED AGAINST BLOCK PREVIOUSLY LAID

MORTAR BED JOINT

GUIDE LINE

Fig. 7. Illustrating common method of picking up and setting concrete block.

61

level, as shown in Fig. 8. In a well constructed wall, mortar joints will average 3/8-inch thick.

Tooling Mortar Joints

When the mortar has become firm, the joints are tooled or finished. Various tools are used for this purpose. A rounded or V-shaped steel jointer is the tool most commonly used, as shown in Fig. 9. Tooling compresses the mortar in the joints, forcing it up tightly against the edges of the block and leaves the joints smooth and watertight. Some joints may be cut off flush and struck with the trowel.

Building Around Door and Window Frames

There are several acceptable methods of building door and window frames in concrete masonry walls. One method used is to set the frames in the proper position in the wall. The frames are then plumbed and carefully braced, after which the walls are

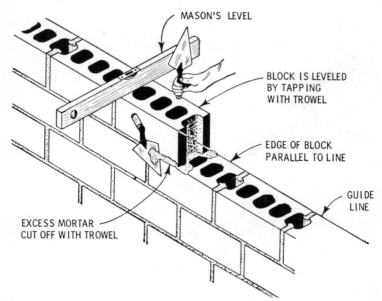

Fig. 8. A method of laying concrete blocks. Good workmanship requires straight courses with face of wall plumb and true.

built up against them on both sides. Concrete sills may be poured later.

The frames are often fastened to the walls with anchor bolts passing through the frames and embedded in the mortar joints. Another method of building frames in concrete masonry walls is to build openings for them, using special jamb blocks, as shown in Fig. 10. The frames are inserted after the wall is built. The only advantage to this method is that the frames can be taken out without damaging the wall, should it ever become necessary.

Placing Sills and Lintels

Building Codes require that concrete block walls above openings shall be supported by arches or lintels of metal or masonry (plain or reinforced). The arches or lintels must extend into the walls not less than 4-inches on each side. Stone or other non-

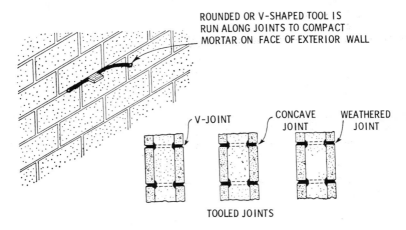

Fig. 9. *Method of tooling to compact mortar between concrete blocks.*

reinforced masonry lintels should not be used unless supplemented on the inside of the wall with iron or steel lintels. Fig. 11 illustrates typical methods of inserting concrete reinforced lintels to provide for door and window openings.

These are usually prefabricated, but may be made up on the job if desired. Lintels are reinforced with steel bars placed 1 1/2-

inches from the lower side. The number and size of reinforcing rods depend upon the width of the opening and the weight of the load to be carried.

Sills serve the purpose of providing watertight bases at the bottom of wall openings. Since they are made in one piece, there are no joints for possible leakage of water into the walls below. They are sloped on the top face to drain water away quickly. They are usually made to project 1 1/2 to 2-inches beyond the wall

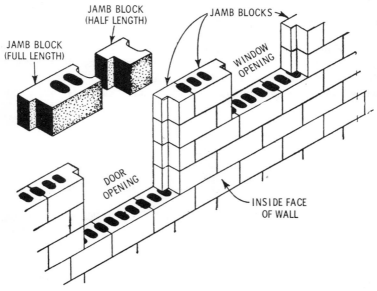

Fig. 10. A method of laying openings for doors and windows.

face, and are made with a groove along the lower outer edge to provide a drain so that water dripping off the sill will fall free and not flow over the face of the wall causing possible staining.

Slip sills are popular because they can be inserted after the wall has been built, and therefore require no protection during construction. Since there is an exposed joint at each end of the sill, special care should be taken to see that it is completely filled with mortar and the joints packed tight.

Lug sills are projected into the concrete block wall (usually 4-in. at each end). The projecting parts are called *lugs*. There are no vertical mortar joints at the juncture of the sills and the jambs. Like the slip sill, lug sills are usually made to project from 1 1/2

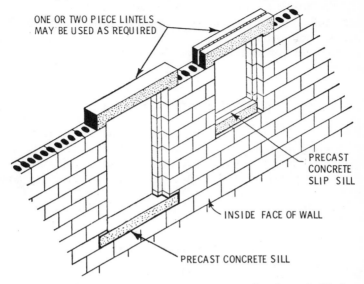

ONE OR TWO PIECE LINTELS MAY BE USED AS REQUIRED

PRECAST CONCRETE SLIP SILL

INSIDE FACE OF WALL

PRECAST CONCRETE SILL

Fig. 11. A method of inserting precast concrete lintels and sills in concrete block walls.

to 2-inches over the face of the wall. The sill is provided with a groove under the lower outer edge to form a drain. Frequently they are made with washes at either end to divert water away from the juncture of the sills and the jambs. This is in addition to the outward slope on the sills.

At the time the lug sills are set, only the portion projecting into the wall is bedded in mortar. The portion immediately below the wall opening is left open and free of contact with the wall below. This is done in case there is minor settlement or adjustments in the masonry work during construction, thus avoiding possible damage to the sill during the construction period.

BASEMENT WALLS

These walls shall not be less in thickness than the walls immediately above them, and not less than 12 inches for unit masonry walls. Solid cast-in-place concrete walls are reinforced with at least one 3/8-in. deformed bar (spaced every 2 ft.) continuous from the footing to the top of the foundation wall. Basement walls with 8-inch hollow concrete blocks frequently prove very troublesome. All hollow-block foundation walls should be capped with a 4-inch solid concrete block, or the core should be filled with concrete.

BUILDING INTERIOR WALLS

Interior walls are built in the same manner as exterior walls. Load-bearing interior walls are usually made 8 inches thick; partition walls that are not load bearing are usually 4 inches thick. The recommended method of joining interior load-bearing walls to exterior walls is illustrated in Fig. 12.

BUILDING TECHNIQUES

Sills and plates are usually attached to concrete block walls by means of anchor bolts, as shown in Fig. 13. These bolts are placed in the cores of the blocks, and the cores filled with concrete. The bolts are spaced about 4 feet apart under average conditions. Usually 1/2-inch bolts are used and should be long enough to go through two courses of blocks and project through the plate about an inch to permit the use of a large washer and the anchor-bolt nut.

Installation of Heating and Ventilating Ducts

These are provided for as shown on the architect's plans. The placement of the heating ducts depends upon the type of wall, whether it is load bearing or not. A typical example of placing the heating or ventilating ducts in an interior concrete masonry wall is shown in Fig. 14.

Interior concrete block walls which are not load bearing, and which are to be plastered on both sides, are frequently cut through to provide for the heating duct, the wall being flush with the ducts on either side. Metal lath is used over the ducts.

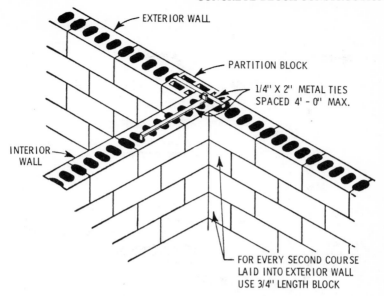

EXTERIOR WALL

PARTITION BLOCK

1/4" X 2" METAL TIES
SPACED 4' - 0" MAX.

INTERIOR
WALL

FOR EVERY SECOND COURSE
LAID INTO EXTERIOR WALL
USE 3/4" LENGTH BLOCK

Fig. 12. Showing detail of joining interior and exterior wall in concrete block construction.

Electrical Outlets

These are provided for by inserting outlet boxes in the walls as shown in Fig. 15. All wiring should be installed to conform with the requirements of the National Electrical Code and the local Codes in the area.

Fill Insulation

In masonry construction, insulation is provided by filling the cores of concrete block units in all outside walls with granulated insulation as construction proceeds. This filling is usually done in the manner shown in Fig. 16 when the walls reach the sill line, lintel, and floor line.

Rigid wall board may be placed over 2-inch furring strips attached to the inside of the wall. A 2-inch blanket of insulation can be placed between the furring strips before installing the wall board, as shown in Fig. 16.

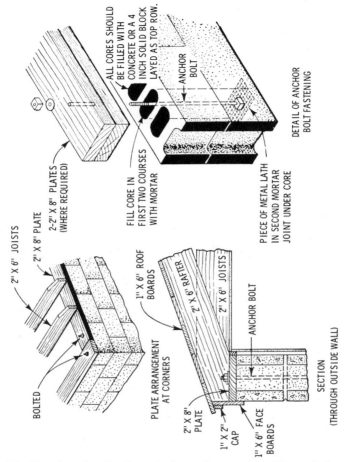

Fig. 13. Showing details of methods used to anchor sills and plates to concrete block walls.

Flashing

Adequate flashing with rust and corrosion-resisting material is of the utmost importance in masonry construction, since it prevents water from getting through the walls at vulnerable points. Points requiring protection by flashing are: Tops and sides of projecting trim; under coping and sills; at intersection of wall and roof; under

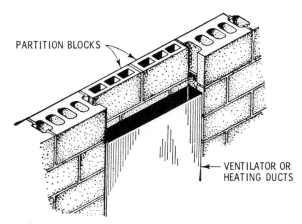

PARTITION BLOCKS

VENTILATOR OR
HEATING DUCTS

Fig. 14. Illustrating method of installing ventilating and heating duct in concrete block walls.

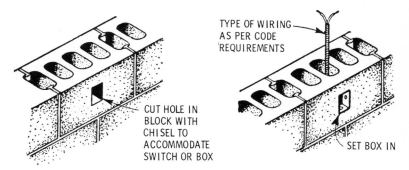

TYPE OF WIRING
AS PER CODE
REQUIREMENTS

CUT HOLE IN
BLOCK WITH
CHISEL TO
ACCOMMODATE
SWITCH OR BOX

SET BOX IN

Fig. 15. Method showing installation of electrical switches and outlet boxes in concrete block walls.

built-in gutters; at intersection of chimney and roof; and at all other points where moisture is likely to gain entrance. Flashing material usually consists of No. 26 gauge (14-oz.) copper sheet or other approved noncorrodable material.

BLOCK AND BRICK WALLS

Concrete blocks and face bricks provide a suitable combination. Cost can often be reduced by laying the blocks with only the

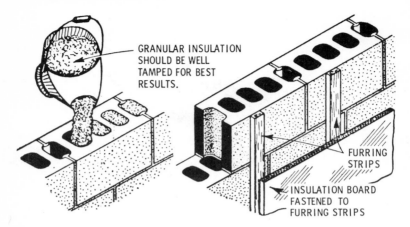

Fig. 16. Method of insulation with granular material, or furring the walls and using blanket type insulation.

front tier of brick, and using clay tile or concrete blocks for the inner tiers. Fig. 17 illustrates the method of laying hollow concrete blocks in backing up an 8- and 12-inch wall. Concrete blocks laid in this manner provide a solid and economical wall.

Since common face brick units are approximately 2 2/3 × 3 3/4 × 8-inches in size, it requires three brick courses to one course of the concrete blocks. This allows for cross bonding every seventh course. Most building Codes require the facing and backing of concrete-block walls to be bonded with either at least one full header course in each seven courses, or with at least one full length header in each 1 1/2 square feet of wall surface. The distance between adjacent full length headers should not, in any event, exceed 20-inches either vertically or horizontally. Where two or more hollow units are used to make up the thickness of a wall, the stretcher courses shall be bonded at vertical intervals not exceeding 34 inches, by lapping at least 3 3/4 inches over the unit below.

In cavity walls, the facing and backing shall be securely tied together with suitable bonding ties of adequate strength, as shown in Fig. 18. A steel rod, 3/16-inch in diameter, or a metal tie of equivalent stiffness (coated with a non-corroding metal or other approved protective coating), shall be used for each 3 sq. ft. of wall surface. Where hollow masonry units are laid with the cells

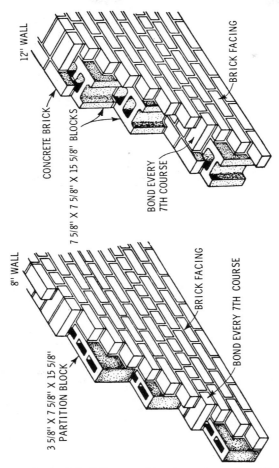

Fig. 17. *A method of building combination masonry walls with brick and 4 and 8 inch concrete blocks.*

vertical, rectangular ties shall be used; in other walls, the ends of the ties shall be bent to 90° angles to provide hooks not less than 2 inches long. Ties shall be embedded in the horizontal joints of the facing and backing. Additional bonding ties shall be provided at all openings, spaced not more than 3 feet apart around the perimeter and within 12 inches of the opening.

71

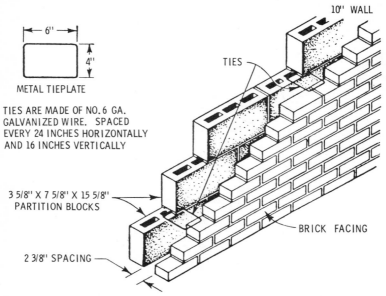

10'' WALL

TIES

METAL TIEPLATE

TIES ARE MADE OF NO. 6 GA.
GALVANIZED WIRE. SPACED
EVERY 24 INCHES HORIZONTALLY
AND 16 INCHES VERTICALLY

3 5/8'' X 7 5/8'' X 15 5/8''
PARTITION BLOCKS

BRICK FACING

2 3/8'' SPACING

Fig. 18. Metal ties used in bonding masonry walls of concrete block and brick.

FLOORS

In concrete masonry construction, floors may be made entirely of wood or concrete, although a combination of concrete and wood is sometimes used. Wooden floors (Fig. 19) must be framed with one governing consideration; they must be made strong enough to carry the load. The type of building and its use will determine the type of floor used, the thickness of the sheathing, and approximate spacing of the joists. The girder is usually made of heavy timber and used to support the lighter joists between the outside walls.

Concrete Floors

There are usually two types of concrete floors—cast-in-place concrete, and precast-joists used with cast-in-place or precast concrete units.

Cast-in-Place—Cast-in-place concrete floors, such as shown

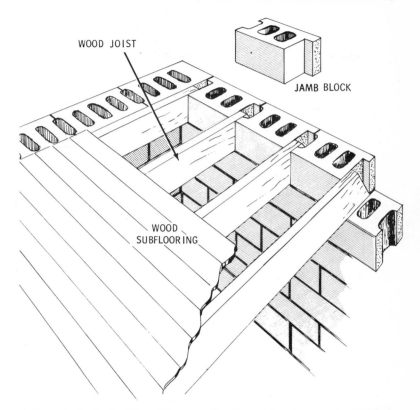

WOOD JOIST

JAMB BLOCK

WOOD
SUBFLOORING

Fig. 19. Method of installing wooden floor joists in concrete blocks.

in Fig. 20, are used in basements, and in residences without basements, and are usually reinforced by means of wire mesh to provide additional strength and to prevent cracks in the floor. This type of floor is used for small areas, such as a porch floor.

Another type of cast-in-place concrete floor is shown in Fig. 21. This floor has more strength because of the built-in joist, and can be used for larger areas.

Precast-Joists—Fig. 22 shows the precast-joist type. The joists are set in place, the wooden forms inserted, the concrete floor is poured, and the forms are removed. Another type of precast-joist concrete floor (Fig. 23) consists of precast concrete joists covered

73

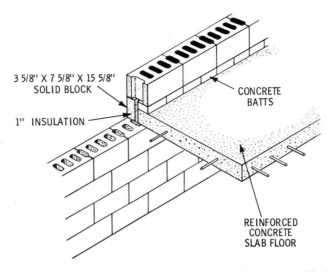

3 5/8" X 7 5/8" X 15 5/8"
SOLID BLOCK

CONCRETE
BATTS

1" INSULATION

REINFORCED
CONCRETE
SLAB FLOOR

Fig. 20. Cast-in-place concrete floor supported by the concrete block wall.

with cast-in-place concrete slabs. The joists are usually made in a concrete products plant.

Usual spacing of the joists is from 27 to 33 inches, depending upon the span and the load. The cast-in-place concrete slab is usually 2- or 2 1/2-inches thick, and extends down over the heads of the joists about 1/2-in. Precast concrete joists are usually made in 8-, 10-, and 12-in. depths. The 8-in. joists are used for spans up to 16 ft., the 10-in. joists are for spans between 16 and 20 ft., and the 12-in. joists are for spans from 20 to 24 ft.

Where masonry partitions that are not load bearing are placed parallel to the joists, it is customary to double the joists under the partition. If the partition runs at right angles to the joists, the usual practice is to design the floor to carry an additional load of 20 lbs. per sq. ft. Precast concrete joists may be left exposed on the underside and painted, or a suspended ceiling may be used. An attractive variation in exposed joist treatment is to double the joists and increase the spacing. Where this is done, the concrete slab is made 2 1/2-inches thick for spacings up to 48 inches, and 3-inches thick for spacings from 48 up to 60 inches. Joists may be doubled by setting them close together or by leaving a space between them and filling the space with concrete.

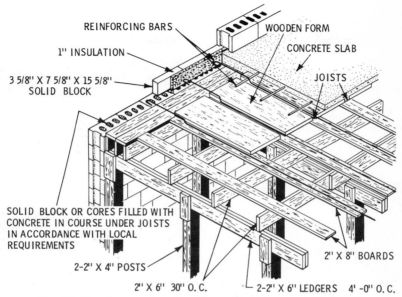

REINFORCING BARS

WOODEN FORM

CONCRETE SLAB

1" INSULATION

JOISTS

3 5/8" X 7 5/8" X 15 5/8"
SOLID BLOCK

SOLID BLOCK OR CORES FILLED WITH
CONCRETE IN COURSE UNDER JOISTS
IN ACCORDANCE WITH LOCAL
REQUIREMENTS

2" X 8" BOARDS

2-2" X 4" POSTS

2" X 6" 30" O. C.

2-2" X 6" LEDGERS   4' -0" O. C.

Fig. 21. Framing construction for cast-in-place concrete floor.

Wood Floors

Where wood-surfaced floors are desired in residences, any type of hardwood, such as maple, birch, beech, or oak may be laid over the structural concrete floor. The standard method of laying hardwood flooring over a structural concrete floor slab is to nail the boards to 2 $\times$ 2 or 2 $\times$ 3-in. sleepers. These sleepers may be tied to the tops of the stirrups protruding from the precast concrete joists. They should be placed not over 16-inches on center, preferably 12-inches in residential construction. Before the hardwood flooring is nailed to the sleepers, the concrete floor must be thoroughly hardened and free from moisture. It is also best to delay laying the hardwood floors until after the plasterers have finished work.

Certain types of parquet and design wood floorings are laid directly on the concrete, being bonded to the surface with bituminous cement. The concrete surface should be troweled smooth

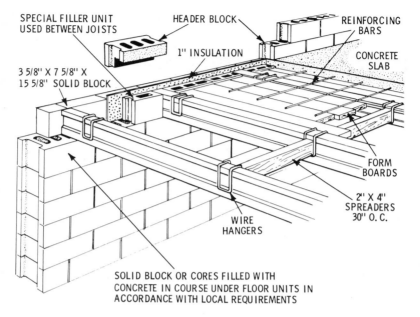

SPECIAL FILLER UNIT
USED BETWEEN JOISTS

HEADER BLOCK

REINFORCING
BARS

1" INSULATION

CONCRETE
SLAB

3 5/8" X 7 5/8" X
15 5/8" SOLID BLOCK

FORM
BOARDS

2" X 4"
SPREADERS
30" O. C.

WIRE
HANGERS

SOLID BLOCK OR CORES FILLED WITH
CONCRETE IN COURSE UNDER FLOOR UNITS IN
ACCORDANCE WITH LOCAL REQUIREMENTS

Fig. 22. Illustrating framing of precast concrete floor joists.

and be free from moisture. No special topping is required; the ordinary level sidewalk finish provides a satisfactory base. Manufacturer's directions for laying this type of wood flooring should be followed carefully in order to insure satisfactory results in the finished floor.

SUMMARY

Concrete blocks provide a very good building material. Blocks are very reasonable in cost, are durable, light weight, fire resistive, and can carry heavy loads. The thickness of concrete blocks is generally 8 inches (except for partition blocks) which is generally specified as the minimum thickness for all exterior walls and for load-bearing interior walls. Partitions and curtain walls are often made 3, 4, or 6 inches thick.

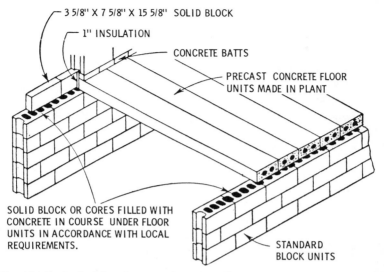

Fig. 23. Method of framing cored concrete floor units into concrete walls.

Concrete blocks are made in several sizes and shapes. For various openings, such as windows or doors, a jamb block is generally used to adapt to various frame designs. Building codes require that concrete-block walls above openings shall be supported by arches of steel or pre-cast masonry lintels. Lintels are usually prefabricated, but may be made on the job if desired. They are reinforced with steel bars placed approximately 1½-inches from the lower side.

Brick and concrete blocks provide a suitable combination, and the cost of a wall can be reduced by laying the blocks with the bricks into some very attractive patterns. A solid 8- or 12-inch wall can be constructed in this manner at an economical cost.

In concrete-block construction, floors may be entirely of wood or concrete, although a combination of the two materials is sometimes used. Wooden joist may be installed into the block wall by using jamb blocks or by installing a sill plate at the top of the wall. Concrete floors are generally of the cast-in-place, precast units, or precast-joist types.

REVIEW QUESTIONS

1. What is the general thickness of concrete blocks?
2. What is the standard measurements of a full-size concrete block?
3. What are lintels? Why are they used?
4. How are combination concrete-block and brick walls constructed?
5. What are precast joists?

CHAPTER 5

Framing

KNOWLEDGE OF LUMBER

The basic construction material in carpentry is lumber. There are numerous kinds of lumber varying greatly in structural characteristics. This book deals with the various types of lumber common to construction carpentry, its application, the standard sizes in which it is available, and the methods of computing lumber quantities in terms of *board feet*.

Standard Sizes of Bulk Lumber

Lumber is usually sawed into standard lengths, widths, and thickness. This permits uniformity in planning structures and in ordering material. Table 1 lists the common widths and thickness of wood in rough, and in dressed dimensions in the United States. Standards have been established for dimension differences between nominal size and the standard size, (which is actually the reduced size when dressed). It is important that these dimension differences be taken into consideration when planning a structure. A good example of the dimension difference may be illustrated by the common 2 × 4. As may be seen in the table, the familiar quoted sixe (2 × 4) refers to a rough or nominal dimension, but the actual standard size to which the lumber is dressed is 1½ × 3½ inches.

Grades of Lumber

Lumber as it comes from the sawmill is divided into three main classes; yard lumber, structural material, and factory or shop

TABLE 1. Your Guide to New Sizes of Lumber

WHAT YOU ORDER	WHAT YOU GET		WHAT YOU USED TO GET
	* Dry or Seasoned	** Green or Unseasoned	Seasoned or Unseasoned
1 x 4	3/4 x 3 1/2	25/32 x 3 9/16	25/32 x 3 5/8
1 x 6	3/4 x 5 1/2	25/32 x 5 5/8	25/32 x 5 1/2
1 x 8	3/4 x 7 1/4	25/32 x 7 1/2	25/32 x 7 1/2
1 x 10	3/4 x 9 1/4	25/32 x 9 1/2	25/32 x 9 1/2
1 x 12	3/4 x 11 1/4	25/32 x 11 1/2	25/32 x 11 1/2
2 x 4	1 1/2 x 3 1/2	1 9/16 x 3 9/16	1 5/8 x 3 5/8
2 x 6	1 1/2 x 5 1/2	1 9/16 x 5 5/8	1 5/8 x 5 1/2
2 x 8	1 1/2 x 7 1/4	1 9/16 x 7 1/2	1 5/8 x 7 1/2
2 x 10	1 1/2 x 9 1/4	1 9/16 x 9 1/2	1 5/8 x 9 1/2
2 x 12	1 1/2 x 11 1/4	1 9/16 x 11 1/2	1 5/8 x 11 1/2
4 x 4	3 1/2 x 3 1/2	3 9/16 x 3 9/16	3 5/8 x 3 5/8
4 x 6	3 1/2 x 5 1/2	3 9/16 x 5 5/8	3 5/8 x 5 1/2
4 x 8	3 1/2 x 7 1/4	3 9/16 x 7 1/2	3 5/8 x 7 1/2
4 x 10	3 1/2 x 9 1/4	3 9/16 x 9 1/2	3 5/8 x 9 1/2
4 x 12	3 1/2 x 11 1/4	3 9/16 x 11 1/2	3 5/8 x 11 1/2

*19% Moisture Content or under.

**Over 19% Moisture Content.

lumber. In keeping with the purpose of this book, only yard lumber will be considered. Yard lumber is manufactured and classified, on a quality basis, into sizes, shapes, and qualities required for ordinary construction and general building purposes. It is then further subdivided into classifications of select lumber and common lumber.

Select Lumber—Select lumber is of good appearance and finished or dressed. It is identified by the following grade names:

Grade A. Grade A is suitable for natural finishes, of high quality, and is practically clear.

Grade B. Grade B is suitable for natural finishes, of high quality, and is generally clear.

Grade C. Grade C is adapted to high quality paint finish.

Grade D. Grade D is suitable for paint finishes, and is between the higher finishing grades and the common grades.

Common Lumber—Common lumber is suitable for general construction and utility purposes, and is identified by the following grade name:

No. 1 common. No. 1 common is suitable for use without waste. It is sound and tight knotted, and may be considered water-tight material.

No. 2 common. No. 2 common is less restricted in quality than No. 1, but of the same general quality. It is used for framing, sheathing, and other structural forms where the stress or strain is not excessive.

No. 3 common. No. 3 common permits some waste with prevailing grade characteristics larger than in No. 2. It is used for such rough work as footings, guardrails, and rough subflooring.

No. 4 common. No. 4 common permits waste, and is of low quality, admitting the coarsest features such as decay and holes. It is used for sheathing, subfloors, and roof boards in the cheaper types of construction. The most important industrial outlet for this grade is for boxes and shipping crates.

No. 5 common. No. 5 common is not produced in some species. The only requirement is that it must be usable for boxes and crates.

FRAMING LUMBER

The frame of a building consists of the wooden form constructed to support the finished members of the structure. It includes such items as posts, girders (beams), joists, sub-floor, sole plate, studs, and rafters. Soft woods are usually used for lightwood framing, and all other aspects of construction carpentry considered in this book. One of the classifications of soft wood lumber cut to standard sizes is called yard lumber, and is manufactured for general building purposes. It is cut into the standard sizes required for light framing, including 2×4, 2×6, 2×8, 2×10, 2×12, and all other sizes required for framework, with the exception of those sizes classed as structural lumber.

Although No. 1 and No. 3 common are sometimes used for framing, No. 2 common is most often used, and is therefore most often stocked and available in retail lumber yards in the common sizes for various framing members. However, the size of lumber required for any specific structure will vary with the design of the building, such as light-frame, heavy-frame etc., and the design of the particular members such as beams or girders.

The exterior walls of a frame building usually consist of three layers—sheathing, building paper, and siding. Sheathing lumber is usually 1×6's or 1×8's, No. 2 or No. 3 common soft wood. It may be plain, tongue-and-groove, or ship lapped. The siding lumber may be grade C, which is most often used. Siding is usually procured in bundles consisting of a given number of square feet per bundle, and come in various lengths up to a maximum of 20 feet.

COMPUTING BOARD FEET

The arithmetic method of computing the number of board feet in one or more pieces of lumber is by the use of the following formula:

$$\frac{\text{Pieces} \times \text{Thickness (inches)} \times \text{Width (inches)} \times \text{Length (feet)}}{12}$$

Example 1—Find the number of board feet in a piece of lumber 2-inches thick, 10-inches wide, and 6-feet long.

$$\frac{1 \times 2 \times 10 \times 6}{12} = 10 \text{ board feet.}$$

Example 2—Find the number of board feet in 10 pieces of lumber 2-inches thick, 10-inches wide, and 6-feet long.

$$\frac{10 \times 2 \times 10 \times 6}{12} = 100 \text{ board feet.}$$

Example 3—Find the number of board feet in a piece of lumber 2-inches thick, 10-inches wide, and 18-inches long.

$$\frac{2 \times 10 \times 18}{144} = 2 \ 1/2 \text{ board feet.}$$

(NOTE: If all three dimensions are expressed in inches, the

same formula applies except the divisor is changed to 144.)

The tabular method of computing board feet with the use of a framing square is covered in Chapter 23 "How to Use the Steel Square" in *Carpenters and Builders Guide No. 1*.

METHODS OF FRAMING

Good material and workmanship will be of very little value unless the underlying framework of a building is strong and rigid. The resistance of a house to such forces as tornadoes and earthquakes, and control of cracks due to settlement, all depends on a good framework.

Although it is true that no two buildings are put together in exactly the same manner, disagreement exists among architects and carpenters as to which method of framing will prove most satisfactory for a given condition. *Light framed construction* may be classified into three distinct types known as:

1. Balloon frame.
2. Braced frame.
3. Western frame (sometimes identified as platform-frame).

Balloon Frame Construction

The principle characteristics of *balloon framing* is the use of studs extending in one piece from the foundation to the roof, as shown in Fig. 1. The joists are nailed to the studs and also supported by a ledger board set into the studs. Diagonal sheathing may be used instead of wall board to eliminate corner bracing.

Braced Frame Construction

The *braced frame construction* is said to be the oldest method of framing in this country, having been imported from England in colonial times. Although in a somewhat modified form, it is still being used in certain states, notably in the east. Originally, this type of framing was characterized by heavy timber posts at the corners, as shown in Fig. 2, and often with intermediate posts between, which extended continuously from a heavy foundation sill to an equally heavy plate at the roof line.

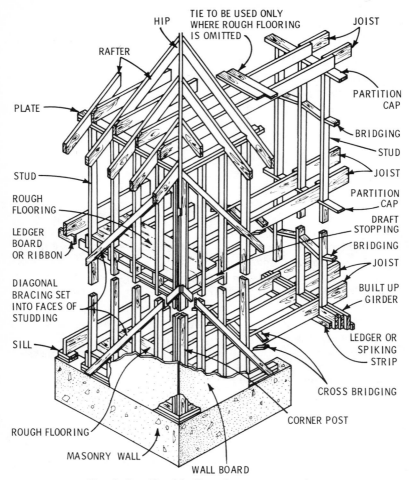

PLATE

RAFTER

HIP

TIE TO BE USED ONLY
WHERE ROUGH FLOORING
IS OMITTED

JOIST

PARTITION
CAP

BRIDGING

STUD

JOIST

PARTITION
CAP

DRAFT
STOPPING

BRIDGING

JOIST

BUILT UP
GIRDER

LEDGER OR
SPIKING
STRIP

STUD

ROUGH
FLOORING

LEDGER
BOARD
OR RIBBON

DIAGONAL
BRACING SET
INTO FACES OF
STUDDING

SILL

ROUGH FLOORING

MASONRY WALL

WALL BOARD

CROSS BRIDGING

CORNER POST

Fig. 1. Details of balloon frame construction.

Western Frame Construction

This type of framing is characterized by platforms independently framed, the second or third floor being supported by the studs from the first floor, as shown in Fig. 3. The chief advantage in this type of framing (in all-lumber construction), lies in the fact that

84

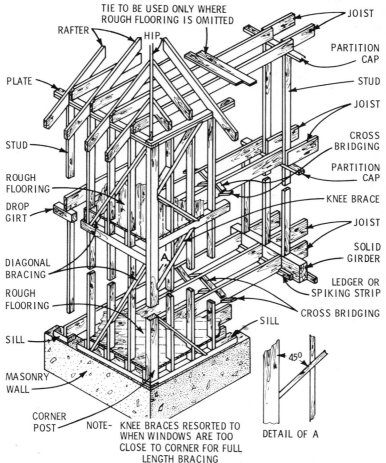

TIE TO BE USED ONLY WHERE
ROUGH FLOORING IS OMITTED

RAFTER

HIP

PLATE

STUD

ROUGH
FLOORING

DROP
GIRT

DIAGONAL
BRACING

ROUGH
FLOORING

SILL

MASONRY
WALL

CORNER
POST

JOIST

PARTITION
CAP

STUD

JOIST

CROSS
BRIDGING

PARTITION
CAP

KNEE BRACE

JOIST

SOLID
GIRDER

LEDGER OR
SPIKING STRIP

CROSS BRIDGING

SILL

A

45°

DETAIL OF A

NOTE— KNEE BRACES RESORTED TO
WHEN WINDOWS ARE TOO
CLOSE TO CORNER FOR FULL
LENGTH BRACING

Fig. 2. Details of bracèd frame construction.

if there is any settlement due to shrinkage, it will be uniform throughout and will not be noticeable.

FOUNDATION SILLS

The foundation sill consists of a plank or timber resting upon

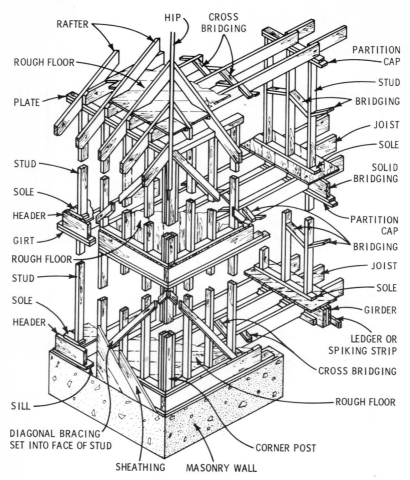

RAFTER

HIP

CROSS BRIDGING

ROUGH FLOOR

PLATE

STUD

SOLE

HEADER

GIRT

ROUGH FLOOR

STUD

SOLE

HEADER

SILL

DIAGONAL BRACING SET INTO FACE OF STUD

SHEATHING   MASONRY WALL

PARTITION CAP

STUD

BRIDGING

JOIST

SOLE

SOLID BRIDGING

PARTITION CAP

BRIDGING

JOIST

SOLE

GIRDER

LEDGER OR SPIKING STRIP

CROSS BRIDGING

ROUGH FLOOR

CORNER POST

Fig. 3. Details of Western frame construction.

the foundation wall. It forms the support or bearing surface for the outside of the building and, as a rule, the first floor joists rest upon it. Shown in Fig. 4 is the balloon-type construction of first and second floor joist and sills. In Fig. 5 is shown the joist and sills used in braced-type framing, and in Fig. 6 is shown the western-type construction.

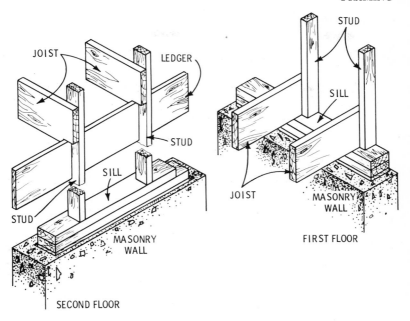

Fig. 4. Details of balloon framing of sill plates and joists.

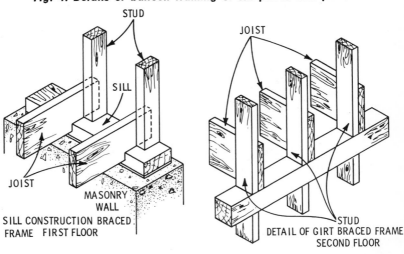

Fig. 5. Details of braced framing of sill plates and joists.

87

Size of Sills

The size of sills for small buildings of light frame construction consists of 2 × 6-inch lumber, which has been found to be large enough under most conditions. For two-story buildings, and especially in locations subject to earthquakes or tornadoes, a double sill is desirable, as it affords a larger nailing surface for

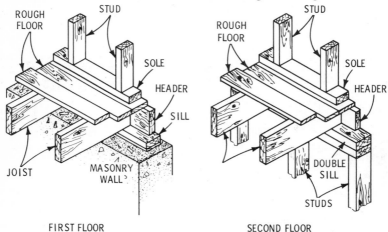

BOX-SILL CONSTRUCTION WESTERN FRAME

Fig. 6. Details of Western framing of sill plates and joists.

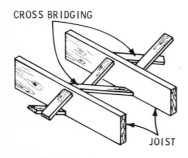

Fig. 7. Cross bridging between floor joists.

CROSS-BRIDGING BETWEEN JOISTS

diagonal sheathing brought down over the sill, and ties the wall framing more firmly to its sills. In cases where the building is supported by posts or piers, it is necessary to increase the sill size, since the sill supported by posts acts as a girder. In balloon framing, for example, it is customary to build up the sills with two or more planks 2 or 3 inches thick, which are nailed together.

In most types of construction, since it is not necessary that the sill be of great strength, the foundation will provide uniform solid bearing throughout its entire length. The main requirements are: resistance to crushing across the grain; ability to withstand decay and attacks of insects; and to furnish adequate nailing area for studs, joists, and sheathing.

Length of Sill

The length of the sill is determined by the size of the building, and hence the foundation should be laid out accordingly. Dimension lines for the outside of the building are generally figured from the outside face of the subsiding or sheathing, which is about the same as the outside finish of unsheathed buildings.

Anchorage of Sill

It is important, especially in locations of strong winds, that buildings be thoroughly anchored to the foundation. Anchoring is accomplished by setting at suitable intervals (6- to 8-feet) 1/2-inch bolts that extend at least 18 inches into the foundation. They should project above the sill to receive a good size washer and nut. With hollow tile, concrete blocks, and material of cellular structure, particular care should be taken in filling the cells in which the bolts are placed solidly with concrete.

Splicing of Sill

As previously stated, a 2 $\times$ 6-inch sill is large enough for small buildings under normal conditions, if properly bedded on the foundations. In order to properly accomplish the splicing of a sill, it is necessary that special precaution be taken. A poorly fitted joint weakens rather than strengthens the sill frame. Where the sill is built up of two planks, the joints in the two courses should be staggered.

Placing of Sill

It is absolutely essential that the foundation be level when placing the sill. It is considered a good practice to spread a bed of mortar on the top foundation blocks and lay the sill upon it at once, tapping it gently to secure an even bearing throughout its length. The nuts of the anchoring bolts can then be put in place over the washers and tightened lightly. The nut is securely tightened only after the mortar has had time to harden. In this manner a good bearing of the sill is provided, which prevents air leakage between the sill and the foundation wall.

GIRDERS

A girder in small house construction consists of a large beam at the first story line, which takes the place of an interior foundation wall and supports the inner ends of the floor joists. In a building where the space between the outside walls is more than 14 to 15 feet, it is generally necessary to provide additional support near the center to avoid the necessity of excessively heavy floor joists. When a determination is made as to the number of girders and their location, consideration should be given to the required length of the joists, to the room arrangement, as well as to the location of the bearing partitions.

LENGTH OF JOISTS

In ordinary cases one girder will generally be sufficient, but if the joist span exceeds 15 feet, a 2 × 10-inch joist is usually required, making necessary another girder.

Bridging Between Joists

Cross bridging consists of diagonal pieces (usually 1 × 3 or 1 × 4 inches) formed in an X pattern and arranged in rows running at right angles to the joists, as shown in Fig. 7. Their function is to provide a means of stiffening the floors and to distribute the floor load equally. Each piece should be nailed with two or three nails at the top, with the lower ends left loose until the sub-flooring is in place.

Solid bridging is sometimes used in place of cross bridging. Solid bridging serves the same function as cross bridging, but is made of solid lumber the size of the joist, Fig. 8.

Fig. 8. Solid bridging between joist.

INTERIOR PARTITIONS

An interior partition differs from an outside partition, in that it seldom rests on a solid wall. Its supports therefore require careful consideration, making sure they are large enough to carry the required weight. The various interior partitions may be bearing or nonbearing, and may run at either right angles or parallel to the joists upon which they rest.

Partitions Parallel to Joists

Here the entire weight of the partition will be concentrated upon one or two joists, which perhaps are already carrying their full share of the floor load. In most cases, additional strength should be provided. One method is to provide double joists under such partitions—to put an extra joist beside the regular ones. Computation shows that the average partition weighs nearly three times as much as a single joist should be expected to carry. The usual (and approved method) is to double the joists under nonbearing partitions. An alternative method is to place a joist on each side of the partition.

Partitions at Right Angles to Joists

For nonbearing partitions, it is not necessary to increase the size or number of the joists. The partitions themselves may be braced, but even without bracing, they have some degree of rigidity.

PORCHES

All porches not resting directly upon the ground are always supported by various posts or piers which are termed *porch supports*. Unless porches are entirely enclosed, and of two or more stories in height, their weight will not require a massive foundation.

In pier foundations used to carry concentrated loads, the following sizes will be sufficient:

For very small porches, such as stoops 4- to 6-feet square, concrete footings 12-inches square and 6-inches thick should be used.

For the usual type of front or side porch, the supports of which are not over 10 feet apart, concrete footings 18-inches square and 8-inches thick should be used.

For large porches (especially if they are enclosed), the piers of which exceed a 10-foot spacing, footings 21- or 24-inches square and 10- or 12-inches thick should be used.

Large enclosed porches, especially if more than one story, should have footings and foundations similar to those of the main building.

Porch Joists

Porch joists differ from floor joists, because of their need for greater weather resisting qualities due to their exposed location. In order that rain water may run off freely, the porch should slope approximately 1/8-inch per foot away from the wall of the building. Since there is no subfloor, this requires the flooring to run in the direction of the slope (at right angles to the wall). Otherwise, water will stand on the floor wherever there are slight irregularities.

This construction requires an arrangement comprising a series of girders running from the wall to the piers. The joists run at right angles to these girders and rest on top, or are cut in between them. To protect the tops of the joists from rot, place a strip of 45-lb. roofing on the top edge under the flooring.

FRAMING AROUND OPENINGS

It is necessary that some parts of the studs be cut out around windows or doors in outside walls or partitions. It is imperative to insert some form of a header to support the lower ends of the top studs that have been cut off. There is a member that is termed a rough sill at the bottom of the window openings. This sill serves as a nailer, but does not support any weight.

HEADERS

Headers are of two classes, namely:

1. Nonbearing headers which occur in the walls which are parallel with the joists of the floor above, and carry only the weight of the framing immediately above.
2. Load-bearing headers, in walls which carry the end of the floor joists either on plates or rib bands immediately above the openings, and must therefore support the weight of the floor or the floors above.

Size of Headers

The determining factor in header sizes is whether they are load bearing or not. In general, it is considered good practice to use a double 2 × 4 header placed on edge unless the opening in a nonbearing partition is more than 3-feet wide. In cases where the trim inside and outside is too wide to prevent satisfactory nailing over the openings, it may become necessary to double the header to provide a nailing base for the trim.

CORNER STUDS

These are studs which occur at the intersection of two walls at right angles to each other. A satisfactory arrangement of corner studs is shown in Fig. 9.

ROOFS

Generally, it may be said that rafters serve the same purpose for a roof as joists do for the floors. They provide a support for sheathing and roof material. Among the various kinds of rafters used, regular rafters extending without interruption from the eave to the ridge are the most common.

Spacing of Rafters

Spacing of rafters is determined by the stiffness of the sheathing between rafters, by the weight of the roof, and by the rafter span. In most cases, the rafters are spaced 16 or 24 inches on center.

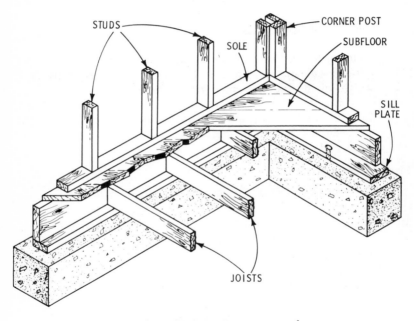

STUDS

CORNER POST

SOLE

SUBFLOOR

SILL PLATE

JOISTS

Fig. 9. Detail view of a corner stud.

Size of Rafters

The size of the rafters will depend upon the following factors:

1. The span.
2. The weight of the roof material.
3. The snow and wind loads.

Span of Rafters

In order to avoid any misunderstanding as to what is meant by the span of a rafter, the following definition is given:

The *rafter span* is the horizontal distance between the supports and not the overall length from end to end of the rafter. The span may be between the wall plate and the ridge, or from outside wall to outside wall, depending on the type of roof.

Length of Rafters

Length of rafters must be sufficient to allow for the necessary cut at the ridge and to allow for the protection of the eaves as determined by the drawings used. This length should not be confused with the span as used for determining strength.

Collar Beams

Collar beams may be defined as ties between rafters on opposite sides of a roof. If the attic is to be utilized for rooms, collar beams may be lathed as ceiling rafters, providing they are spaced properly. In general, collar beams should not be relied upon as ties. The closer the ties are to the top, the greater the leverage action. There is a tendency for the collar beam nails to pull out, and also for the rafter to bend if the collar beams are too low. The function of the collar beam is to stiffen the roof. These beams are often, although not always, placed at every rafter. Placing them at every second or third rafter is usually sufficient.

Size of Collar Beams

If the function of a collar beam were merely to resist a thrust, it would be unnecessary to use material thicker than 1-inch lumber. But, as stiffening the roof is their real purpose, the beams must have sufficient body to resist buckling, or else must be braced to prevent bending.

HIP RAFTERS

The hip roof is built in such a shape that its geometrical form is that of a pyramid, sloping down on all four sides. A hip is formed where two adjacent sides meet. The hip rafter is the one which runs from the corner of the building upward along the same plane of the common rafter. Where hip rafters are short and the upper

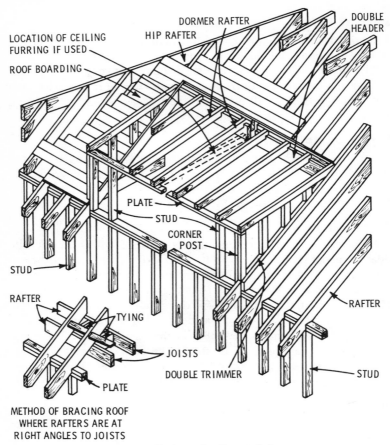

LOCATION OF CEILING FURRING IF USED

ROOF BOARDING

DORMER RAFTER

HIP RAFTER

DOUBLE HEADER

PLATE

STUD

CORNER POST

STUD

RAFTER

TYING

JOISTS

DOUBLE TRIMMER

PLATE

RAFTER

STUD

METHOD OF BRACING ROOF WHERE RAFTERS ARE AT RIGHT ANGLES TO JOISTS

Fig. 10. Detail view of a flat roof dormer.

ends come together at the corner of the roof (lending each other support), they may safely be of the same size as that of the regular rafters.

For longer spans, however, and particularly when the upper end of the hip rafter is supported vertically from below, an increase of size is necessary. The hip rafter will necessarily be slightly wider than the jacks, in order to give sufficient nailing surface. A properly sheathed hip roof is nearly self-supporting. It is the strongest roof of any type of framing in common use.

DORMERS

The term *dormer* is given to any window protruding from a roof. The general purpose of a dormer may be to provide light or to add to the architectural effect.

In general construction, there are three types of dormers, as follows:

1. Dormers with flat sloping roofs, but with less slope than the roof in which they are located, as shown in Fig. 10.

2. Dormers with roofs of the gable type at right angles to the roof.

3. A combination of the above types, which gives the hip-type former (Fig. 11).

When framing the roof for a dormer window, an opening is provided in which the dormer is later built in. As the spans are usually short, light material may be used.

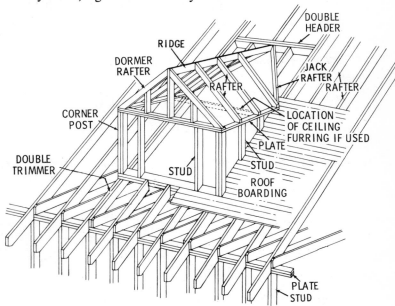

Fig. 11. Detail view of a hip roof dormer.

STAIRWAYS

The well built stairway is something more than a convenient means of getting from one floor to another. It must be placed in the right location of the house. The stairs themselves must be so designed that traveling up or down can be accomplished with the least amount of discomfort.

The various terms used in stairway building are as follows:

1. The *rise* of a stairway is the height from the top of the lower floor to the top of the upper floor.
2. The *run* of the stairs is the length of the floor space occupied by the construction.
3. The *pitch* is the angle of inclination at which the stairs run.
4. The *tread* is that part of the horizontal surface on which the foot is placed.
5. The *riser* is the vertical board under the front edge of the tread.
6. The *stringers* is the frame work on the sides which are cut to support the steps.

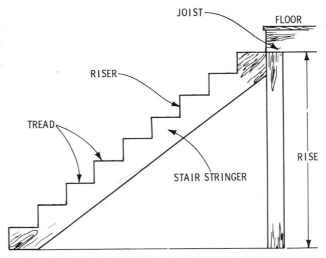

Fig. 12. A method of laying out stair stringers showing the rise and tread.

A commonly followed rule in stair construction is that the *tread* should not measure less than 9 inches, and the *riser* should not be more than 8-inches high, as shown in Fig. 12. The width measurement of the tread and height of the riser combined should not exceed 17 inches. Measurements are the cuts of the strings, not the actual width of the boards used for risers and treads. Treads usually have a projection, called a *nosing,* beyond the edge of the riser.

FIRE AND DRAFT STOPS

It is known that many fires originate in the basement. It is therefore important that fire stops be provided in order to prevent a fire from spreading through the building by way of air passages between the studs. Similarly, fire stops should be provided at each floor level to prevent flames from spreading through the walls and partitions from one floor to the next. Solid blocking should be provided between joists and studs to prevent fire from passing across the building.

In the Western frame and braced frame, the construction itself provides stops at all levels. In this type of construction, therefore, fire-stops are needed only in the floor space over the bearing partitions. Masonry is sometimes utilized for fire stopping, but is usually adaptable in only a few places. Generally, obstructions in the air passages may be made of 2-inch lumber, which will effectively prevent the rapid spread of fire. Precautions should be made to insure the proper fitting of fire stops throughout the building.

CHIMNEY AND FIREPLACE CONSTRUCTION

Although the carpenter is ordinarily not concerned with the building of the chimney, it is necessary, however, that he be acquainted with the methods of framing around the chimney.

The following minimum requirements are recommended:

1. No wooden beams, joists, or rafters shall be placed within 2 inches of the outside face of a chimney. No woodwork shall be placed within 4 inches of the back wall of any fireplace.
2. No wooden studding, furring, lathing, or plugging should be placed against any chimney or in the joints thereof. Wood-

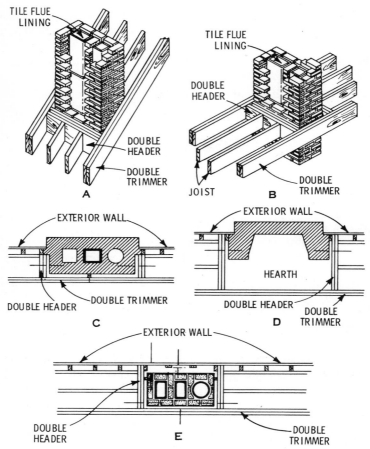

Fig. 13. Framing around chimneys and fireplaces; A. Roof framing around chimney; B. Floor framing around chimney; C. Framing around chimney above fireplace D. Floor framing around fireplace; E. Framing around concealed chimney above fireplace.

en construction shall either be set away from the chimney or the plastering shall be directly on the masonry or on metal lathing or on incombustible furring material.

3. The walls of fireplaces shall never be less than 8-inches thick if of brick, or 12-inches if built of stone.

Formerly, it was advised to pack all spaces between chimneys and wood framing with incombustible insulation. It is now known that this practice is not as fire-resistant as the empty air-spaces, since the air may carry away dangerous heat while the insulation may become so hot that it becomes a fire-hazard itself. Fig. 13 shows typical framing around chimneys and fireplaces.

SUMMARY

Lumber is usually milled into standard lengths, widths, and thickness. It is important that these dimensions be taken into consideration when planning a structure. Lumber shipped from the sawmill is divided into three main classes, namely, yard lumber, structural lumber, and factory or shop lumber. Yard lumber is used for house framing and is identified by grades.

Sill plates rest upon the foundation walls and are generally anchored down with bolts embedded in the foundation wall at approximately 6- to 8-foot intervals. These bolts should project above the sill plate to receive a large-size washer and nut. The sill plate is usually placed on a fresh bed of mortar and tapped gently in place to secure an even bearing seat throughout the length of the sill.

Framing for a building consists of such items as posts, girders, beams, joists, subfloor, sole plates, studs, and rafters. Each particular phase of framing must meet with good material and workmanship to withstand such forces as tornadoes and earthquakes, and control of cracks due to settlement of the foundation. Balloon, braced, and western framing are three distinct methods of construction.

REVIEW QUESTIONS

1. Name the three types of light frame construction.
2. How are sill plates anchored to the foundation walls?
3. What items are included in framing a building?
4. How is board feet computed?
5. What is cross bridging between floor joists, and why is it so important?

CHAPTER 6

Framing Terms

SILLS

The sills are the first part of the framing to be set in place. Sills may rest either directly on foundation piers or other type of foundation, and usually extend all around the building. Where double or built-up sills are used, the joints are staggered and the corner joints are lapped, as shown in Fig. 1. When box sills are used, that part of the sill that rests on the foundation wall is called the sill plate.

GIRDERS

A girder may be either a single beam or a composite section. Girders usually support joists, whereas the girders themselves are supported by bearing walls or columns. When a girder is supported by a wall or pier, it must be remembered that such a girder delivers a large concentrated load to a small section of the wall or pier. Therefore, care must be taken to see that the wall or pier is strong enough to carry the load imposed upon it by the girder. Girders are generally used only where the joist will not safely span the distance. The size of a girder is determined by the span length and the load to be carried.

JOISTS

Joists are the pieces which make up the body of the floor frame, and to which the flooring and subflooring is nailed (see Fig. 2).

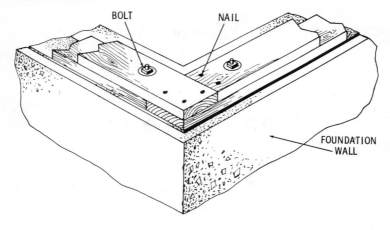

Fig. 1. Details of a double or built-up sill construction.

They are usually 2- or 3-inches thick with a varying depth to suit conditions. Joists are usually considered to carry a uniform load composed of the weight of the joists themselves, in addition to the flooring and the weight of furniture and persons.

SUBFLOORING

A subfloor, if used, is usually laid diagonally on the joists and properly nailed to them, as shown in Fig. 3. By the use of sub-flooring, floors are made much stronger since the floor weight is distributed over a larger area. It may be laid before or after the walls are framed, but preferably before. The subfloor can then be used as a floor to work on while framing the walls. The material for subflooring can be 1 × 6-inch sheathing boards or plywood.

HEADERS AND TRIMMERS

A girder is often necessary when an opening is to be made in a floor. The timbers on each side of such an opening are called *trimmers,* and these must be made heavier than ordinary joists. A piece called a *header* must be framed in between the trimmers to receive the ends of the short joists.

104

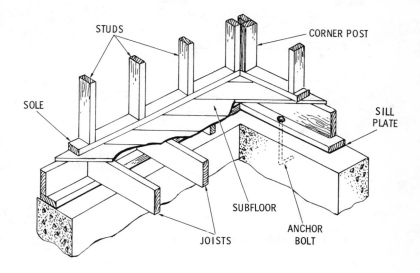

STUDS

CORNER POST

SOLE

SILL PLATE

SUBFLOOR

ANCHOR BOLT

JOISTS

Fig. 2. Detail view of floor joists and subfloor.

WALLS

All walls and partitions in which the structural elements are wood are classed as *frame construction.* Their structural elements are usually closely spaced, and contains a number of slender vertical members termed *studs.* These are arranged in a row with their ends bearing on a long longitudinal member called the *bottom plate* or *sole plate,* and their tops capped with another plate called the *top plate.* The bearing strength of the stud walls is governed by the length of the studs.

CORNER POSTS

After the sill and first floor joists are in place, the corner posts are set up, plumbed, and temporarily braced. The corner post may be made in several different ways, depending upon the size and construction of the building.

105

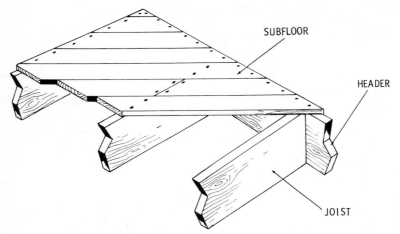

Fig. 3. Method of laying wooden subflooring.

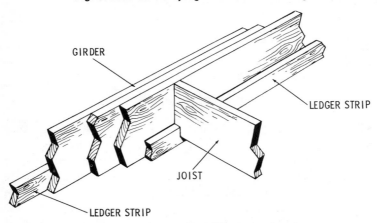

Fig. 4. Detail of girder and method of supporting joists by using a ledger strip.

LEDGER PLATES

In connecting joists to girders and sills where piers are used, a 2 × 4-inch piece is nailed to the face of the sill or girder and flush with the bottom edge, as shown in Fig. 4. This is called a *ledger*.

TOP PLATES AND SOLE PLATES

The top plate serves two purposes—to tie the studding together at the top and form a finish for the walls, and to furnish a support for the lower end of the rafters. The top plate further serves as a connecting link between the ceiling and the walls.

The plate is made up of one or two pieces of timber of the same size as the studs. In cases where studs at the end of the building extend to the rafters, no plate is used. When it is used on top of partition walls, it is sometimes called a *cap*. The *sole plate* is the bottom horizontal member on which the studs rest.

BRACES

Braces are used as a permanent part of the structure. They tend to stiffen the walls and to keep corners square and plumb. Braces also prevent the frame from being distorted by lateral forces, such as wind or by settlement. These braces are placed wherever the sills or plates make an angle with the corner post, or with a T-post in the outside wall. The brace extends from the sill or sole plate to the top of the post, forming an angle of approximately 60 degrees with the sole plate and an angle of 30 degrees with the post.

STUDS

After the sills, posts, plates, and braces are in place, the studs are installed and nailed to the top plate. Before the studs are set in place, the windows and door openings are laid out. Then the remaining or intermediate studs are laid out on the sills or soles by measuring from one corner and spacing them the correct distance apart. In some instances, the studs are nailed to the top and sill plates while the entire assembly is resting flat on the floor. The wall is then raised into position.

Studs are set from one to several feet apart, depending upon the type of building and the type of outside and inside finish. Where vertical siding is used, studs are set wider apart since the horizontal girts between them afford the nailing surface.

PARTITION WALLS

Partition walls are any walls that divide the inside space of a building. In most cases, these walls are framed as a part of the building. In cases where floors are to be installed after the outside of the building is completed, the partition walls are left unframed. There are two types of partition walls, the *bearing* and *nonbearing*. The bearing type supports ceiling joists. The nonbearing type supports only itself, and may be put in at any time after the framework is installed. Only one cap or plate is used.

A sole plate should be used in every case as it helps to distribute the load over a large area. Partition walls are framed in the same manner as outside walls, and inside door openings are framed the same as outside openings. Where there are corners (or where one partition wall joins another), corner posts or T-posts are used in the outside walls. These posts provide nailing surfaces for the inside wall finish.

BRIDGING

Walls of frame buildings are bridged in most cases to increase their strength. There are two methods of bridging, the *diagonal* and the *horizontal*. Diagonal bridging is nailed between the studs at an angle. It is more effective than the horizontal type since it forms a continuous truss and tends to keep the walls from sagging. Whenever possible, both outside and inside walls should be bridged alike.

Horizontal bridging is nailed between the studs and halfway between the sole and top plate. This bridging is cut to lengths which correspond to the distance between the studs at the bottom. Such bridging not only stiffens the wall but will also help straighten the studs.

RAFTERS

In all roofs, the pieces which make up the main body of the framework are called the *rafters*. They do for the roof what the joists do for the floor or the studs do for the wall. The rafters are inclined members usually spaced from 16 to 24 inches on center, which rest at the bottom on the plate and are fastened on center at the top in various ways according to the form of the roof. The plate forms the connecting link between the wall and the roof and is really a part of both.

The size of the rafters varies, depending upon the length and the distance at which they are spaced. The connection between the rafter and the wall is the same in all types of roofs. They may or may not extend out a short distance from the wall to form the eaves and to protect the sides of the building.

SUMMARY

After the foundation walls have been completed, the first part of framing is to set the sills in place. The sills are usually placed on a bed of fresh mortar to ensure a tight seal, and usually extend all around the building. Where double or built-up sills are used, the joints are staggered and the corner joints are lapped.

Where floor joists span a large distance, girders are used to help support the load. The size of a girder depends on the span length of the joists. Girders may be either a steel I-beam or can be built on the job from 2 × 8 or 2 × 10 lumber placed side by side.

Joists are the pieces which make up the body of the floor frame, and to which the subflooring is nailed. The joists are usually 2 × 6 or 2 × 8 lumber commonly spaced 16 or 24 inches apart. The subflooring is generally installed before the wall construction is started, and in this manner the subfloor can serve as a work floor.

REVIEW QUESTIONS

1. Explain the purpose of the sill plate, floor joists, and girder.
2. What is the purpose of the subflooring?
3. What is a ledger strip?
4. What is a sole plate?
5. Where are headers and trimmers used?

CHAPTER 7

Girders and Sills

Chapter 5 gave a general idea of the several classes of frames. The various details of these frames vary greatly. There are many ways of constructing each part and, in this connection, purchasers or those contemplating having a house built should be acquainted not only with the right construction methods, but also with the methods that are objectionable.

It is poor economy to specify inexpensive and inferior construction as houses so built are often not satisfactory. In this and following chapters the various parts of the frame, such as *girders, sills, corner posts, studding, etc.,* are considered in detail, showing the numerous ways in which each part is treated.

GIRDERS

By definition, a *girder* is *a principal beam extending from wall to wall of a building affording support for the joists or floor beams where the distance is too great for a single span.* Girders may be either solid or built up, as shown in Figs. 1 and 2.

Construction of Girders

Girders can be built up of wood if select stock is used. Be sure it is straight and sound. If the girders are to be built up of 2 $\times$ 8 or 2 $\times$ 10 stock, place the pieces on the sawhorses and nail them together. Use the pieces of stock that has the least amount of warp for the center piece and nail other pieces on the sides of

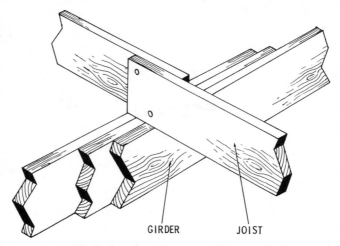

Fig. 1. Ilustration of girders and joists construction.

the center stock. Use a common nail that will go through the first piece and nearly through the center piece. Square off the ends of the girder after the pieces have been nailed together. If the stock is not long enough to build up the girder the entire length, the pieces must be built up by staggering the joints. If the girder supporting post is to be built up, it is to be done in the same manner as described for the girder.

Table 1 gives the size of built-up wood girders for various loads and spans, based on Douglas fir 4-square framing lumber.

All girders are figured as being made with 2-inch dressed stock. The 6-inch girder is figured three pieces thick; the 8-inch girder four pieces thick; the 10-inch girder with five pieces thick, and the 12-inch girder with six pieces thick. For solid girders multiply the load in Table 1 by 1.130 when 6-inch girders are used; 1.150 when 8-inch girders are used; 1.170 when 10 inch is used, and 1.180 when 12-inch girders are used.

Placing Basement Girders

Basement girders must be lifted into place on top of the piers and walls built for them, and set perfectly level and straight from end to end. Some carpenters prefer to give the girders a slight

BOLTS   IRON PLATE   WOODEN BEAMS

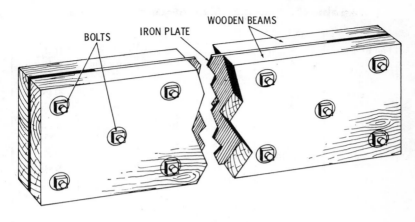

Fig. 2. A flitch plate girder.

crown of approximately 1 inch in the entire length, which is a wise plan, because the piers generally settle more than the outside walls. When there are posts instead of brick piers used to support the girder, the best method is to temporarily support the girder by uprights made of 2×4 joists resting on blocks on the ground below. When the superstructure is raised, these can be knocked out after the permanent posts are placed. The practice of temporarily shoring the girders, and not placing the permanent supports until after the superstructure is finished, is favored by good builders, and it is well for carpenters to know just how it should be done. Permanent supports are usually made by using 3- or 4-inch steel pipe set in a concrete foundation, or footing that is at least 12 inches deep.

SILLS

A *sill is that part of the side walls of a house that rests horizontally upon, and* is *securely fastened to, the foundation.* There are numerous types of sills, and some of the creations that now go under the name of sill would not be recognized by an old time workman. In fact, a stretch of the imagination is necessary

113

Table 1. Nominal Size of Girder Required

Load per linear foot of girder	Length of Span				
	6-foot	7-foot	8-foot	9-foot	10-foot
750	6x8 in	6x8 in	6x8 in	6x10 in	6x10 in
900	6x8	6x8	6x10	6x10	8x10
1050	6x8	6x10	8x10	8x10	8x12
1200	6x10	8x10	8x10	8x10	8x12
1350	6x10	8x10	8x10	8x12	10x12
1500	8x10	8x10	8x12	10x12	10x12
1650	8x10	8x12	10x12	10x12	10x14
1800	8x10	8x12	10x12	10x12	10x14
1950	8x12	10x12	10x12	10x14	12x14
2100	8x12	10x12	10x14	12x14	12x14
2250	10x12	10x12	10x14	12x14	12x14
2400	10x12	10x14	10x14	12x14	x
2550	10x12	10x14	12x14	12x14	x
2700	10x12	10x14	12x14	x	x
2850	10x14	12x14	12x14	x	x
3000	10x14	12x14	x	x	x
3150	10x14	12x14	x	x	x
3300	12x14	12x14	x	x	x

to associate some of these modern contrivances with the duty they are supposed to perform.

Sills may be divided into two general classes:

1. Solid.
2. Built up.

The built-up sill has become more or less a necessity because of the scarcity and high cost of timber, especially in the larger sizes. The work involved in sill construction is very important for the carpenter. The foundation wall is the support upon which the entire structure rests. The sill is the foundation on which all the framing structure rests, and is the real point of departure for actual carpentry and joinery activities. The sills are the first part of the frame to be set in place. They either rest directly on the foundation piers or on the ground, and may extend all around the building.

The type of sill used depends upon the general type of construction, and are called:

1. Box sills.
2. T-sills.

3. Braced framing sills.
4. Built-up sills.

Box Sills—Box sills are often used with the very common style of platform framing, either with or without the sill plate. In this type of sill the part that lies on the foundation wall or ground is called the sill plate. The sill is laid edgewise on the outside edge of the sill plate.

T-Sills—There are two types of T-sill construction, one commonly used in the south or dry warm climate, and one used in the north and east where it is colder. Their construction is

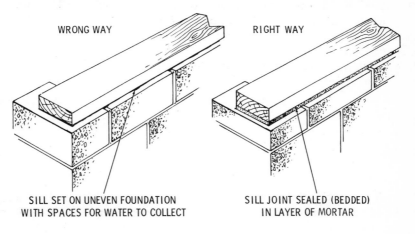

SILL SET ON UNEVEN FOUNDATION   SILL JOINT SEALED (BEDDED)
WITH SPACES FOR WATER TO COLLECT   IN LAYER OF MORTAR

Fig. 3. Wrong and right way to set sills. The top solid block serves as a termite barrier.

similar except in the east the T-sills and joists are nailed directly to the studs, as well as to the sills. The headers are nailed in between the floor joists.

Braced Framing Sills—The floor joists are notched out and nailed directly to the sills and studs.

Built-up Sills—Where built-up sills are used, the joists are staggered. If piers are used in the foundation, heavier sills are used. These sills are of single heavy timber or are built up of two or more pieces of timber. Where heavy timber or built-up type sills are used, the joints should occur over the piers. The size of the

115

sill depends on the load to be carried and on the spacing of the piers. Where earth floors are used, the studs are nailed directly to the sill plates.

Setting the Sills

After the girder is in position, the sills are placed on top of the foundation walls, are fitted together at the joints, and leveled throughout. The last operation can either be done by a sight level, or by laying them in a full bed of mortar and leveling them with the anchor bolts, as shown in Fig. 3.

Sills that are to rest on a wall of masonry should be kept up at least 18 inches above the ground, as decaying sills are a frightful source of trouble and expense in wooden buildings. Sheathing, paper, and siding should therefore be very carefully installed to effectually exclude all wind and wet weather.

SUMMARY

A girder is a principal beam extending from wall to wall of a building to support the joists or floor beams where the distance is too great for a single span. Girders can be made of wood which must be straight and free of knots. Girders are made three, four, five, or six pieces thick, depending on the load per linear foot and length of the girder.

A sill is that part of the side walls of a house that rests horizontally upon, and is securely fastened to, the foundation. The sills are the first part of the framing to be set in place, therefore it is important that the sill be constructed properly and placed properly on the foundation. There are various types of sills used which depend on the type of house construction. The size of the sill depends on the load to be carried and on the spacing of the piers. In some construction, two sill plates are used, one nailed on top of the other.

REVIEW QUESTIONS

1. Why are girders used?
2. What is a flitch plate?
3. How are sills anchored to the foundation?
4. Name the various types of sills constructed.
5. What is the purpose of the sill?

CHAPTER 8

Floor Framing

After the girders and sills have been placed, the next operation consists in sawing to size the floor beams or joists of the first floor, and placing them in position on the sills and girders. If there is a great variation in the size of timbers, it is necessary to cut the joists 1/2 inch narrower than the timber, so that their upper edges will be in alignment. This sizing should be made from the top edge of the joist as shown in Fig. 1. When the joists have been cut to the correct dimension they should be placed upon the sill and girders, and spaced 16 inches between centers, beginning at one side or end of a room. This is done to avoid waste in material.

CONNECTING JOIST TO SILLS AND GIRDERS

Joists are connected to sills and girders by several methods. In modern construction, the method that requires the least time and labor and yet gives the maximum efficiency is used. In joining joists to sills, always be sure that the connection is able to hold the load that the joists will carry.

The framing of the joists to the girders may be accomplished in several ways, depending upon the position of the girders. The placing of the girders is an important factor. The joists must be level; therefore, if the girder is not the same height as the sill, the joists must be notched. In placing joists, always have the crown up since this counteracts the weight on the joists; in most cases there will be no sag below a straight line. When a joist is to rest on plates or girders, the joist is cut long enough to extend the full width of the plate or girder.

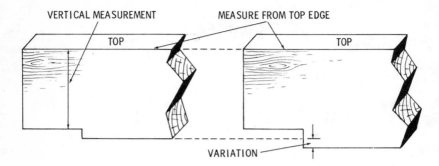

VERTICAL MEASUREMENT   MEASURE FROM TOP EDGE

TOP   TOP

VARIATION

Fig. 1. Showing the variation of joists width.

BRIDGING

To prevent joists springing sideways under load, which would reduce their carrying capacity, they are tied together diagonally by 1 × 3 or 2 × 3 strips. This reinforcement is called *bridging*. The 1 × 3 ties are used for small houses and the 2 × 3 stock on larger work.

Rows of bridging should not be more than 8 feet apart. Bridging pieces may be cut all in one operation with a miter box, or the more common method shown in Fig. 2 may be employed. Bridging is put in before the subfloor is laid, and each piece is fastened with two nails at the top end. The subfloor should be laid before the bottom end is nailed.

A more rigid (less vibrating) floor is made by cutting in solid 2-inch joists of the same depth. They should be cut perfectly square and a little full, say 1/16-inch longer than the inside distance between the joists. First, set one in every other space, then go back and put in the intervening ones. This prevents spreading the joists and allows the second ones to be driven in with the strain the same in both directions. This solid blocking is much more effective than cross-bridging. The blocks should be toenailed end to end, and not staggered and nailed through the joists.

HEADERS AND TRIMMERS

The foregoing operations would complete the first-floor frame-

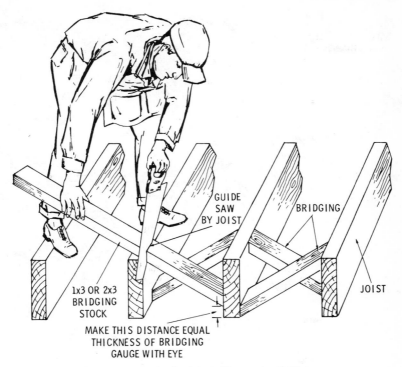

GUIDE SAW BY JOIST

BRIDGING

JOIST

1x3 OR 2x3 BRIDGING STOCK

MAKE THIS DISTANCE EQUAL THICKNESS OF BRIDGING GAUGE WITH EYE

Fig. 2. A method of installing joist bridging.

work in rooms having no framed openings, such as those for stair ways, chimneys, elevators, etc.

The definition of a header is *a short transverse joist which supports the ends of one or more joists (called tail beams) where they are cut off at an opening.* A trimmer is *a carrying joist which supports an end of a header.*

Shown in Fig. 3 are typical floor openings used for chimneys and stairways. For these openings, the headers and trimmers are set in place first, then the floor joists are installed. Hanger irons of the type shown in Fig. 4 are nearly obsolete, but many other types of metal hangers are available, such as the one shown in Fig. 5.

Headers run at right angles to the direction of the joists and are doubled. Trimmers run parallel to the joists and are actually

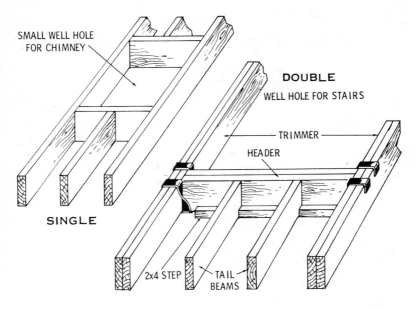

SMALL WELL HOLE
FOR CHIMNEY

DOUBLE

WELL HOLE FOR STAIRS

TRIMMER

HEADER

SINGLE

2x4 STEP   TAIL
BEAMS

Fig. 3. Single and double header and trimmer construction for floor openings.

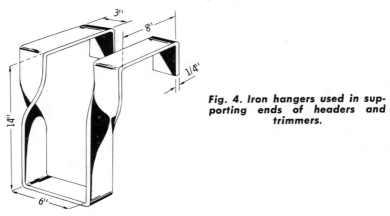

3"

8"

1/4"

14"

6"

Fig. 4. Iron hangers used in supporting ends of headers and trimmers.

doubled joists. The joists are framed to the headers where the headers form the opening frame at right angles to the joists. These shorter joists framed to the headers are called *tail beams*. The

Fig. 5. One of the many types of metal hangers in common use.

number of headers and trimmers required at any opening depends upon the shape of the opening.

SUBFLOORING

With the sills and floor joists completed, it is necessary to install the subflooring. The subflooring is permanently laid before erecting any wall framework, since the wall plate rests on it. In most cases the subfloor is laid diagonally as shown in Fig. 6, to give strength and to prevent squeaks in the floor. This floor is called the rough floor, or subfloor, and may be visioned as a large platform covering the entire width and length of the building. Two layers or coverings of flooring material (subflooring and finished flooring) are placed on the joists. Boards 6 to 8 inches wide are used, or, in some cases, 4 × 8 foot sheets of plywood are used for subflooring.

FINISH FLOORING

A finished floor is in most cases 3/4-inch material, tongue-and-groove, and varies in width. Prefinished flooring can be obtained which will save time and labor. In warehouses, where heavy loads are to be carried on the floor, 2-inch material should be used.

DIAGONAL
SUBFLOORING

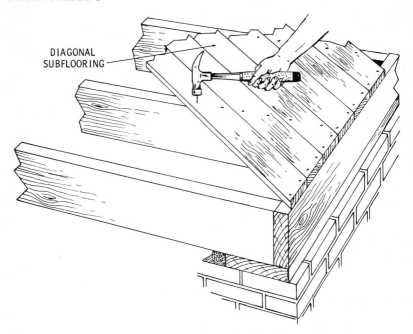

Fig. 6. The subflooring is laid diagonally for greater strength.

SUMMARY

After the sill plate and girder have been constructed and installed, the next operation is to install the floor joists. After cutting the joists to the proper length, the next operation is to check variation in width. If there is a great variation in the size of the timbers, it is necessary to cut or notch out the bottom edge to align the joists.

To prevent joists from warping under load, which would reduce their carrying capacity, they are tied together diagonally with 1 × 3 or 2 × 3 strips called bridging. Bridging is installed before the subflooring is laid, and each piece is fastened with two nails at the top end. The subfloor should be laid before the bottom end is nailed.

124

After the joists are installed, the subflooring is laid. In most cases the subfloor is laid diagonally to give strength and to prevent squeaks in the floor. The material generally used for subfloors is 1 × 6 or 1 × 8 boards, or in some cases 4 × 8-foot sheets of plywood.

The finished floor in most cases is ¾-inch tongue and groove. To save time and labor, a prefinished flooring can be obtained. Where heavy loads are to be carried on the floor, 2-inch flooring should be used.

REVIEW QUESTIONS

1. What must be done to align the top edge of floor joists?
2. What is bridging, and how is it installed?
3. How should subflooring be laid?
4. When are headers and trimmers used in floor joists?
5. What are tail beams?

CHAPTER 9

Outer Wall Framing

Where the construction permits, it is advisable to permanently lay the subfloor before erecting the wall studding. Besides saving time in laying and removing a temporary floor, it also furnishes a surface on which to work and a sheltered place in the basement for storage of tools and materials.

BUILT-UP CORNER POSTS

There is a multiplicity of ways in which corner posts may be built up, using studding or larger sized pieces. Some carpenters form corner posts with two 2 × 4 studs spiked together to make a piece having a 4 × 4 section. Except for very small structures, such a flimsily built-up piece should not be used as a corner post. Fig. 1 shows various arrangements of built-up posts commonly used.

BALLOON BRACING

In balloon framing, the bracing may be temporary or permanent. Temporary bracing means strips nailed on (as in Fig. 2) to hold the frame during construction and are then removed when the permanent bracing is in place. There are two kinds of permanent bracing. One type is called *cut-in* bracing, and is shown in Fig. 3. A house braced in this manner withstood one of the worst hurricanes ever to hit the eastern seaboard, and engineers, after an inspection, gave the bracing the full credit for the survival. The other type of bracing is called *plank* bracing, and is shown in Fig. 4. This type is put on from the outside, the studs being cut and notched so that the bracing is flush with the out-

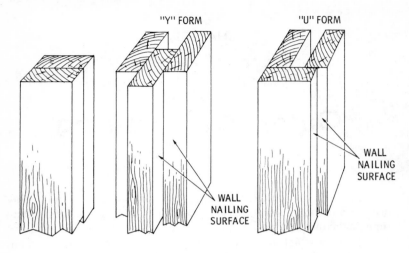

Fig. 1. Various ways to build up corner post.

side edges of the studs. This method of bracing is commonly used and is very effective.

PREPARING THE CORNER POSTS AND STUDDING

In laying out the posts and studs, a pattern should be used to insure that all will be of the same length, with the gains, and any other notches or mortises to be cut, at the same elevation. The pattern can be made from a 7/8-inch board, or a 2 × 4 stud, and must be cut to the exact length and squared at both ends. The pattern should be made from a selected piece of wood having straight edges.

If a stud is selected for the pattern, it may be used later in the building, and thus counted in with the total number of pieces to be framed. The wall studs are placed on their edges on the horses in quantities of 6 to 10 at a time and marked from the pattern, as shown in Fig. 5.

ERECTING THE FRAME

If the builder is short-handed, or working by himself, a frame can be *crippled* together, one member at a time. An experienced

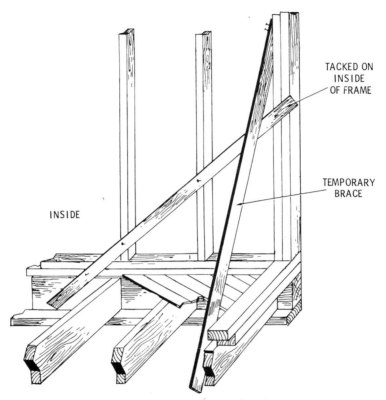

**TACKED ON
INSIDE
OF FRAME**

**TEMPORARY
BRACE**

INSIDE

Fig. 2. Temporary frame bracing.

carpenter can erect the studs and toenail them in place with no assistance whatever. Then the corners are plumbed and the top plates nailed on from a stepladder. Where enough men are available, most contractors prefer to nail the sole plates and top plates as the entire wall is lying down on the rough floor. Some even cut all the door and window openings, after which the entire gang raises the assembly and nails it in position. Needless to say, the platform frame with the subfloor in place is best adapted to this kind of construction. It is probably the speediest of any possible method, but it cannot be done by only one or two men. Some contractors even put on the outside sheathing before raising the wall, and then use a lift truck or a highlift excavating machine to

129

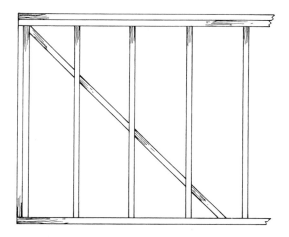

Fig. 3. Permanent 2 x 4 cut between stud bracing. This type of bracing is called cut-in braces.

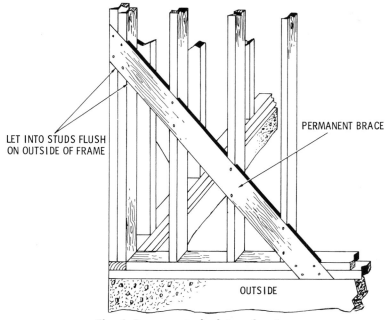

LET INTO STUDS FLUSH
ON OUTSIDE OF FRAME

PERMANENT BRACE

OUTSIDE

Fig. 4. Permanent plank-type bracing.

raise it into position. Each contractor will probably develop his own methods for *saving time,* but the good contractor will also slant his efforts at *improving* the building.

There are many ways to frame the openings for windows and doors. Some builders erect all of the wall studding first, and then cut out the studs for the openings. It is much easier to saw studs lying level on horses than when nailed upright in the frame. The openings should be laid out and framed complete. Studding at all openings must be double to furnish more area for proper nailing of the trim, and must be plumb, as shown in Fig. 6.

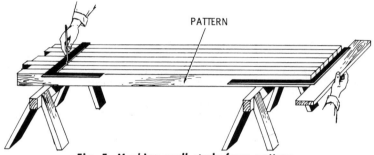

PATTERN

Fig. 5. Marking wall studs from pattern.

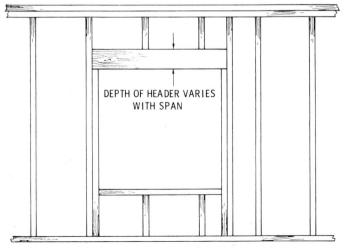

DEPTH OF HEADER VARIES WITH SPAN

Fig. 6. An approved framing for window opening.

OPENING SIZES FOR WINDOWS AND DOORS

Standard double-hung windows are listed by unit dimensions, giving the width first. A 2'-0" × 3'-0" double hung window has an overall glass size of 28½ inches. The rough opening is 2'-10", and the sash opening is 2'-8".

It is common to frame the openings with dimensions 2-inches over the unit dimension. This will allow for the plumbing and leveling of the window.

For door openings, allow a full 1 inch over the door size for the thickness of the jambs, with about 1 inch additional for blocking and plumbing. This will make the opening width 3 inches over the door size. Standard oak thresholds are 5/8-in. thick, making the overall height of the door-frame butt 5/8 inches above the finish floor line. If you wish to allow for the lugs on the frame (which is a good idea), allow 5 inches over the door size for the height of the opening above the finish floor line. Door casings are set to show a slight rabbet, or set back, to allow for clearance of the hinges, while windows are usually cased flush with the inside

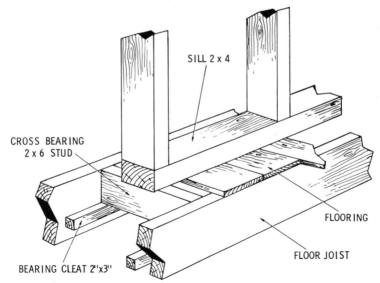

Fig. 7. A method of constructing a partition between two floor joists.

edges of the jambs. If the heights of the window and door head casings are to be the same (as they often are), the window frames must be set the height of this rabbet *higher* than the door frames. Continuous head trim is almost a thing of the past but where it is to be used, the carpenter can easily get into an almost uncorrectable situation if this difference is neglected.

PARTITIONS

Interior walls which divide the inside space of the buildings into rooms, halls, etc., are known as partitions. These are made up of studding covered with plaster board and plaster, metal lath and plaster, or dry wall. Fig. 7 shows the studding of an ordinary partition, each joist being 16 inches on center. Where partitions are placed between and parallel to floor joist, bridges must be placed between the joists to provide a means of fastening the partition plate.

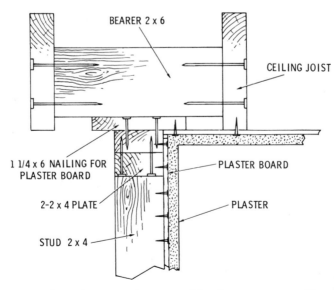

Fig. 8. A method of constructing a partition between two ceiling joists.

133

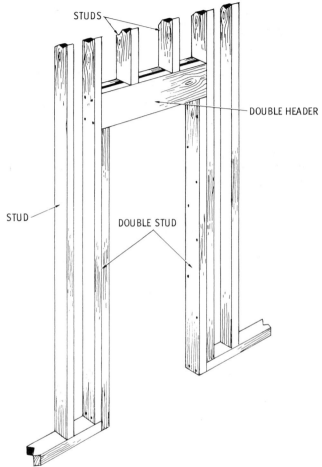

STUDS

DOUBLE HEADER

STUD

DOUBLE STUD

Fig. 9. Construction of headers when openings over 30 inches between studs appear in partitions or outside walls.

The construction at the top is shown in Fig. 8. Openings over 30 inches wide in partitions or outside walls must have heavy headers, as shown in Fig. 9. The partition wall studs are arranged in a row with their ends bearing on a long horizontal member called a bottom plate, and their tops capped with another plate, called a top plate. Double top plates are used in bearing walls and partitions. The bearing strength of stud walls is determined by the strength of the studs.

Walls and partition coverings are divided into two general types—wet-wall material (generally plaster), and dry-wall material including wood, plasterboard, plywood, and fiberboard. Dry-wall material usually comes in 4 × 8 and 4 × 12 foot sheets, and in various thicknesses. It is normally applied in either single or double thickness. When covering both walls and ceiling, always start with the ceiling first.

The size and shape of the ceiling will largely determine which method will be used when installing dry wall. When the number of pieces and their size have been determined, the first thing to do is build two T-braces to hold the panels in place, as shown in Fig. 10. Raise the first panel in position and hold it in place with the T-brackets. Each panel should be nailed at least every 4 inches, starting at the center of the board and working outward. Due to the weight of dry-wall-boards, a special nail can be pur-

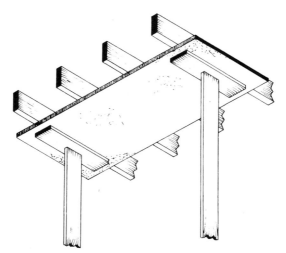

Fig. 10. T-braces used to temporarily support sheets of dry-wall material on the ceiling.

chased which will not pull out and let the ceiling sag. Dimple the nail below the surface of the panel, being careful not to break the surface of the board by the blow of the hammer.

After the ceiling has been installed, start in a corner on the side wall and proceed in the same manner, making sure that all joints break at the center line of a stud. Cut all openings for pipes and electrical receptacles with a keyhole saw. Cover all nail heads with dry-wall cement. Joints may be left open, beveled, lapped, filled, or covered with battens of moulding. If joints are to be filled, the treatment varies slightly with different materials. Generally, all cracks over 1/8 inch wide must be filled with special crack filler before joint cement is applied. The cement is spread over the joints with a plasterer's trowel. Apply the cement evenly and then feather the edges on the surface of the wall panel. Fill channels in recessed edges with cement, carrying it 1 inch past the channel edges. At the corners, apply cement in a channel-wide band and feather the edges. Press perforated tape into the wet cement and smooth the tape down with a trowel. Clean off excess cement. At the corners, fold the tape down the center before applying, and smooth each side of the corner separately. When the cement has dried, apply a second coat of cement to hide the tape. Feather the edges carefully to preserve the flat appearance of the wall. When the final coat of cement is dry, smooth the joints with sandpaper.

SUMMARY

After the subfloor has been laid, the outer wall framing can be erected. There are generally two types of permanent bracing; cut-in and plank, which is a very important part of outer wall framing.

If a carpenter is working alone, he can erect each stud and toenail into the sole plate with no assistance whatsoever. The top plate can be nailed from a stepladder, after the corners and studs are plumb. When enough men are available, most contractors prefer to nail the sole plates and top plates as the entire wall is laying down on the floor or ground. In many cases, all of the door and window openings are constructed and nailed in place, then the wall is raised as one unit and nailed in position.

Interior wall which divide the inside space into rooms, halls, etc., are generally known as partitions. They are made up of studding covered with plaster or plaster board, with each joist being set 16 inches on center. Where partitions are to be placed between and parallel to the floor joists, bridges must be placed between the joists to provide a means of fastening the partition plate.

REVIEW QUESTIONS

1. Why is corner bracing so important?
2. What is the difference between a load-bearing and a nonload-bearing partition?
3. What is a bearer?
4. Why should double headers and studs be installed in door and window openings?
5. Why are corner post designs so important?

CHAPTER 10

Roof Framing

As a preliminary to the study of this chapter, the reader should review Chapter 23 in Vol. 1 on "How to Use the Steel Square." This tool, which is invaluable to the carpenter in roof framing, has been explained at great length in this chapter with numerous examples of rafter cutting. Hence, a knowledge of how to use the square will be assumed here to avoid repetition.

TYPES OF ROOFS

There are numerous forms of roofs and an endless variety of shapes. The carpenter and the student, as well as the architect, should be familiar with the names and features of each of the various types.

Shed or Lean-to Roof

This is the simplest form of roof (shown in Fig. 1), and is usually employed for small sheds and out buildings. It has a single slope and is not a thing of beauty.

Saw-Tooth Roof

This is a development of the shed or lean-to roof, being virtually a series of lean-to roofs covering one building, as in Fig. 2. It is used on factories, principally because of the extra light which may be obtained through windows on the vertical sides.

Gable or Pitch Roof

This is a very common, simple, and efficient form of roof, and

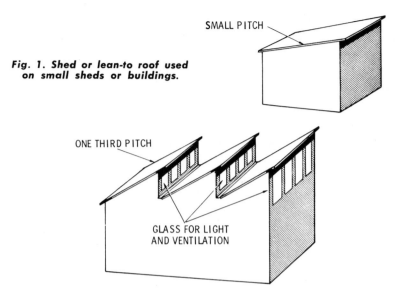

SMALL PITCH

Fig. 1. Shed or lean-to roof used on small sheds or buildings.

ONE THIRD PITCH

GLASS FOR LIGHT
AND VENTILATION

Fig. 2. A sawtooth roof used on factories for light and ventilation.

is used extensively on all kinds of buildings. It is of triangular section, having two slopes meeting at the center or *ridge* and forming a *gable,* as in Fig. 3. It is popular because of the ease of construction, economy, and efficiency.

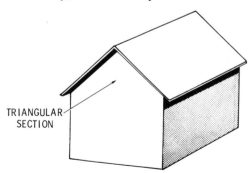

TRIANGULAR
SECTION

Fig. 3. Gable or pitch roof that can be used on all types of buildings.

Gambrel Roof

This is a modification of the gable roof, each side having two slopes, as shown in Fig. 4.

Hip Roof

A hip roof is formed by four straight sides, all sloping toward the center of the building, and terminating in a ridge instead of a deck, as in Fig. 5.

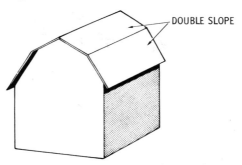

DOUBLE SLOPE

Fig. 4. Gambrel roof used on barns.

Pyramid Roof

A modification of the hip roof in which the four straight sides sloping toward the center terminate in a point instead of a ridge as in Fig. 6. The pitch of the roof on the sides and ends are different. This construction is not often used.

Fig. 5. Hip roof used on all types of buildings.

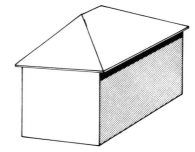

Hip-and-Valley Roof

This is a combination of a hip roof and an intersecting gable roof covering a T- or L-shaped building, as in Fig. 7, and so called because both hip and valley rafters are required in its construction. There are many modifications of this roof. Usually the

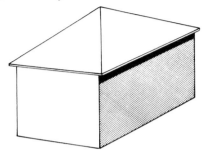

Fig. 6. Pyramid roof which is not often used.

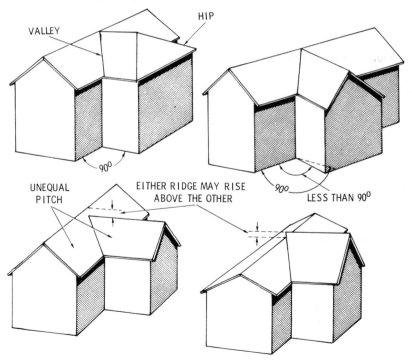

Fig. 7. Various styles of hip and valley roofs.

intersection is at right angles, but it need not be; either ridge may rise above the other and the pitches may be equal or different, thus giving rise to an endless variety, as indicated in Fig. 7.

Double-Gable Roof

This is a modification of a gable or a hip-and-valley roof in which the extension has two gables formed at its end, making an M-shape section, as in Fig. 8.

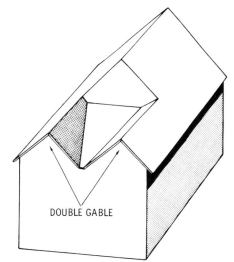

Fig. 8. Double gable roof.

DOUBLE GABLE

Ogee Roof

A pyramidal form of roof having steep sides sloping to the center, each side being ogee-shaped, lying in a compound hollow and round curve, as in Fig. 9.

OGEE CURVE
(COMPOUND)

Fig. 9. Ogee style roof.

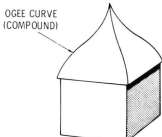

Mansard Roof

The straight sides of this roof slope vary steeply from each side of the building toward the center, and the roof has a nearly flat deck on top, as in Fig. 10. It was introduced by the architect whose name it bears.

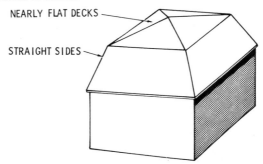

NEARLY FLAT DECKS

STRAIGHT SIDES

Fig. 10. Mansard roof.

French or Concave Mansard Roof

This is a modification of the Mansard roof, its sides being concave instead of straight, as in Fig. 11.

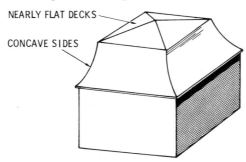

NEARLY FLAT DECKS

CONCAVE SIDES

Fig. 11. French or concave Mansard roof.

Conical Roof or Spire

A steep roof of circular section which tapers uniformly from a circular base to a central point. It is frequently used on towers, as in Fig. 12.

144

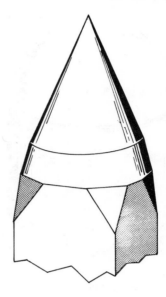

Fig. 12. Conical or spire roof.

Dome

A hemispherical form of roof (Fig. 13) used chiefly on observatories.

ROOF CONSTRUCTION

The frame of most roofs is made up of timbers called rafters. These are inclined upward in pairs, their lower ends resting on the top plate, and their upper ends being tied together with a ridge board. On large buildings, such frame work is usually reinforced by interior supports to avoid using abnormally large timbers.

The primary object of a roof in any climate is to keep out the rain and the cold. The roof must be sloped to shed water. Where heavy snows cover the roof for long periods of time, it must be constructed more rigidly to bear the extra weight. Roofs must also be strong enough to withstand high winds.

The most commonly used types of roof construction includes:

1. Gable.
2. Lean-to or shed.
3. Hip.

145

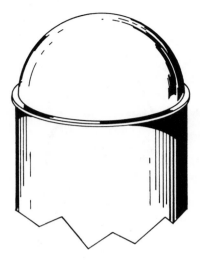

Fig. 13. Dome type roof.

4.. Gable and valley.

Terms used in connection with roofs are, *span, total rise, total run, unit of run, rise in inches, pitch, cut of roof, line length,* and *plumb and level lines.*

Span—The *span* of any roof is the shortest distance between the two opposite rafter seats. Stated in another way, it is the measurement between the outside plates, measured at right angles to the direction of the ridge of the building.

Total Rise—The *total rise* is the vertical distance from the plate to the top of the ridge.

Total Run—The term *total run* always refers to the level distance over which any rafter passes. For the ordinary rafter, this would be one-half the span distance.

Unit of Run—The unit of measurement, 1 foot or 12 inches is the same for the roof as for any other part of the building. By the use of this common unit of measurement, the framing square is employed in laying out large roofs.

Rise in Inches—The *rise in inches* is the number of inches that a roof rises for every foot of run.

Pitch—*Pitch* is the term used to describe the amount of slope of a roof.

Cut of Roof—The *cut of a roof* is the *rise in inches* and *the unit of run* (12 inches).

Line Length—The term *line length* as applied to roof framing is the hypotenuse of a triangle whose base is the total run and whose altitude is the total rise.

Plumb and Level Lines—These terms have reference to the direction of a line on a rafter and not to any particular rafter cut. Any line that is vertical when the rafter is in its proper position is called a *plumb line*. Any line that is level when the rafter is in its proper position is called a *level line*.

RAFTERS

Rafters are the supports for the roof covering and serve in the same capacity as joists do for the floor or studs do for the walls. According to the expanse of the building, rafters vary in size from ordinary 2 × 4's to 2 × 10's. For ordinary dwellings, 2 × 6 rafters are used, spaced from 16 to 24 inches on centers.

The various kinds of rafters used in roof construction are:

1. Common.
2. Hip.
3. Valley.
4. Jack (hip, valley, or cripple).
5. Octagon.

The carpenter should thoroughly know these various types of rafters, and be able to distinguish each kind as they are briefly described.

Common Rafters

A rafter extending at right angles from plate to ridge, as shown in Fig. 14.

Hip Rafter

A rafter extending diagonally from a corner of the plate to the ridge, as shown in Fig. 15.

Valley Rafter

A rafter extending diagonally from the plate to the ridge at the intersection of a gable extension and the main roof.

Jack Rafter

Any rafter which does not extend from the plate to the ridge.

Hip Jack Rafter

A rafter extending from the plate to a hip rafter, and at an angle of 90° to the plate, as shown in Fig. 15.

Valley Jack Rafter

A rafter extending from a valley rafter to the ridge and at an angle of 90° to the ridge, as shown in Fig. 16.

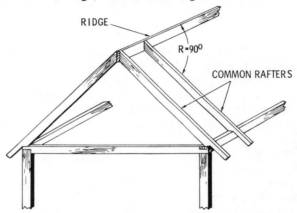

Fig. 14. An illustration of common rafters.

Cripple Jack Rafter

A rafter extending from a valley rafter to hip rafter and at an angle of 90° to the ridge, as shown in Fig. 17.

Octagon Rafter

Any rafter extending from an octagon-shaped plate to a central apex, or ridge pole.

A rafter usually consists of a main part or rafter proper, and a short length called the *tail,* which extends beyond the plate. The rafter and its tail may be all in one piece, or the tail may be a separate piece nailed on to the rafter.

LENGTH OF RAFTER

The length of a rafter may be found in several ways:

1. By calculation.
2. With steel framing square.
   a. Multi-position method.
   b. By scaling.
   c. By aid of the framing table.

Example—What is the length of a common rafter having a run of 6 feet and rise of 4 inches per foot?

1. *By calculation* (See Fig. 18)

The total rise $= 6 \times 4 = 24$ inches $= 2$ feet.

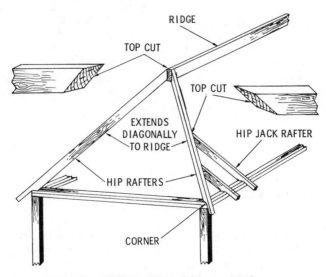

Fig. 15. An illustration of hip roof rafters.

Since the edge of the rafter forms the hypotenuse of a right triangle whose other two sides are the run and rise, then the length of the rafter $= \sqrt{\text{run}^2 + \text{rise}^2} = \sqrt{6^2 + 2^2} = \sqrt{40} = 6.33$ feet, as illustrated in Fig. 18.

149

Practical carpenters would not consider it economical to find rafter lengths in this way, because it takes too much time and there is chance of errors. It is to avoid both of these objections that the *framing square* has been developed.

2. *With steel framing square*

The steel framing square considerably reduces the mental effort and chances of error in finding rafter lengths. An approved method

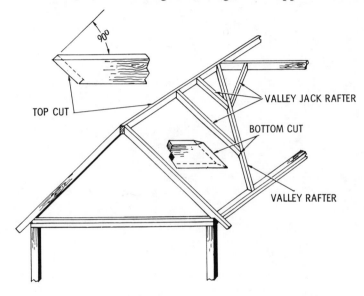

Fig. 16. An illustration of valley and valley jack rafters.

of finding rafter lengths with the square is by the aid of the rafter table included on the square for that purpose. However, some carpenters may possess a square which does not have rafter tables. In such case, the rafter length can be found either by the *multi-position* method shown in Fig. 19, or by *scaling* as in Fig. 20. In either of these methods, the measurements should be made with care because, in the *multi-position* method, a separate measurement must be made for each foot run with a chance for error in each measurement.

Problem: Lay off the length of a common rafter having a run of 6 ft. and a rise of 4-ins. per ft. Locate a point *A* on the edge of the rafter, leaving enough stock for a lookout, if any is used. Place the steel framing square so that division 4 coincides with *A*, and 12 registers with the edge of *B*. Evidently, if the run were 1-ft., distance *AB* thus obtained would be the length of the rafter *per foot run*. Apply the square six times for the 6-ft. run, obtaining points *C, D, E, F,* and *G.* The distance *AG,* then, is the length of the rafter for a given run.

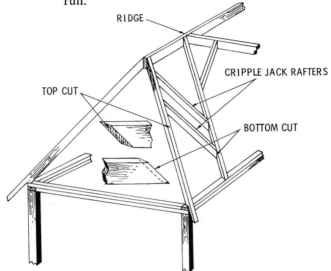

Fig. 17. An illustration of cripple jack rafters.

Fig. 20 shows readings of rafter tables of two well known makes of squares for the length of the rafter in the preceding example, one giving the length per foot run, and the other the total length for the given run.

Problem 1: *Given the rise per ft. in inches.* Use two squares, or a square and a straightedge scale, as shown in Fig. 21. Place the straightedge on the square so

151

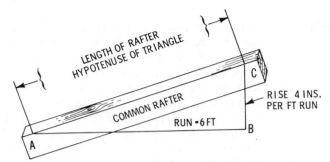

Fig. 18. Method of finding the length of a rafter by calculation.

as to be able to read the length of the diagonal between the rise of 4-ins. on the tongue and the 1-ft. (12-in.) run on the body as shown. The reading is a little over 12 inches. To find the fraction, place dividers on 12 and at point *A,* as in Fig. 22. Transfer to the hundredths scale and read .65, as in Fig. 23, making the length of the rafter 12.65 in. *per ft. run,* which for a 6-ft. run =

$$\frac{12.65 \times 6}{12} = 6.33 \text{ ft.}$$

Problem 2: *Total rise and run given in feet.* Let each inch on the tongue and body of the square = 1 ft. The straightedge should be divided into inches and 12ths of an inch so that on a scale, 1 in. = 1 ft. Each division will therefore equal 1 in. Read the diagonal length between the numbers representing the run and rise (12 and 4), taking the whole number of inches as feet, and the fractions as inches. Transfer the fraction with dividers and apply the 100th scale, as was done in Problem 1, Figs. 22 and 23.

In estimating the total length of stock for a rafter having a tail, the run of the tail or length of the lookout must of course be considered.

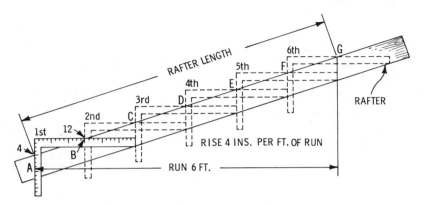

Fig. 19. Multi-position method of finding rafter length.

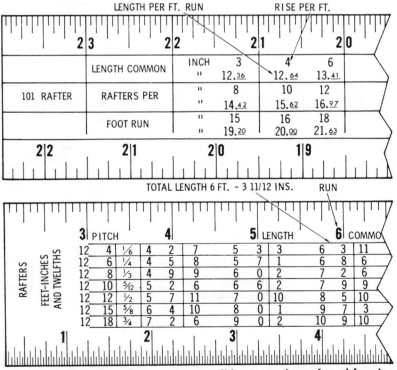

Fig. 20. Rafter table readings of two well-known makers of steel framing squares.

153

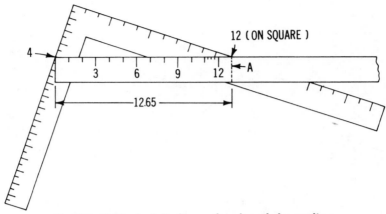

Fig. 21. Method of finding rafter length by scaling.

Fig. 22. Reading the straight edge in combination with the carpenters square.

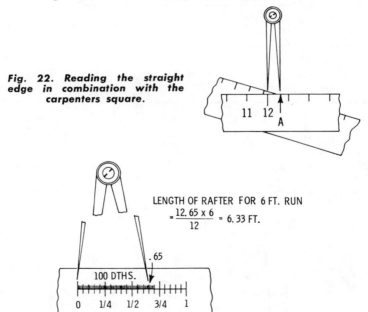

LENGTH OF RAFTER FOR 6 FT. RUN

$$= \frac{12.65 \times 6}{12} = 6.33 \text{ FT.}$$

Fig. 23. Method of reading hundredths scale.

RAFTER CUTS

All rafters must be cut to the proper angle or bevel at the points where they are fastened and, in the case of overhanging rafters, also at the outer end. The various cuts are known as:

1. Top or plumb.
2. Bottom, seat, or heel.
3. Tail or lookout.
4. Side, or cheek.

Common Rafter Cuts

All of the cuts for the various types of common rafters are made at right angles to the sides of the rafter; that is, not beveled as in the case of jacks. Fig. 24 shows various common rafters from which the nature of these various cuts are seen.

In laying out cuts for common rafters, one side of the square is always placed on the edge of the stock at 12, as shown in Fig. 24. This distance 12 corresponds to 1 ft. of the run; the other side of the square is set with the edge of the stock to the rise in inches

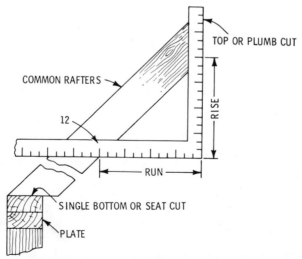

Fig. 24. Various common rafters illustrating types and names of cuts; showing why one side of the square is set at 12 in laying out the cut.

per foot run. This is virtually a repetition of Fig. 19, but it is very important to understand why one side of the square is set to 12 for common rafters—not simply to know that 12 must be used. On rafters having a full tail, as in Fig. 25B, some carpenters do not cut the rafter tails, but wait until the rafters are set in place so that they may be lined and cut while in position. Certain kinds of work permit the ends to be cut at the same time the remainder of the rafter is framed.

The method of handling the square in laying out the bottom and lookout cuts are shown in Fig. 26. In laying out the top or plumb cut, if there is a ridge board, one-half of the thickness of

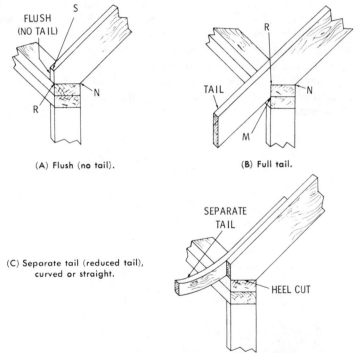

(A) Flush (no tail).

(B) Full tail.

(C) Separate tail (reduced tail),
curved or straight.

Fig. 25. Various forms of common rafter tails.

the ridge must be deducted from the rafter length. If a lookout or a tail cut is to be vertical, place the square at the end of the stock with the rise and run setting as shown in Fig. 26, and scribe the cut line *LF*. Lay off *FS* equal to the length of the look-out, and move the square up to *S* (with the same setting) and scribe line *MS*. On this line, lay off *MR*, the length of the vertical side of the bottom cut. Now apply the same setting to the bottom edge of the rafter, so that the edge of the square cuts *R*, and scribe *RN*, which is the horizontal side line of the bottom cut. In making the bottom cut, the wood is cut out to the lines *MR* and

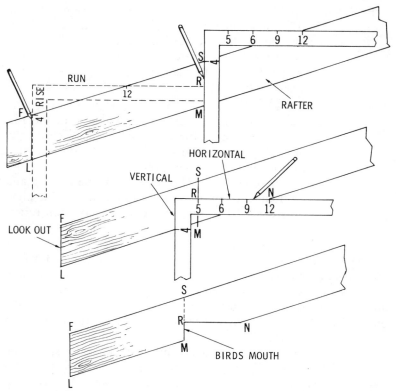

Fig. 26. Method of using the square in laying out the lower or end cut of the rafter.

RN. The lookout and bottom cuts are shown made in Fig. 25B, *RN* being the side which rests on the plate, and *RM* the side which touches the outer side of the plate.

Hip and Valley Rafter Cuts

The hip rafter *lies in the plane of the common rafters* and forms *the hypotenuse of a triangle,* of which one leg is the adjacent common rafter and the other leg is the portion of the plate intercepted between the feet of the hip and common rafters, as in Fig. 27.

Problem: In Fig. 27, take the run of the common rafter as 12, which may be considered as 1 ft. (12 in.) of the run or the total run of 12 ft. (1/2 the span). Now for 12 ft., intercept on the plate the hip run inclined to 45° to the common run, as in the triangle ABC. Thus, $AC^2 = \sqrt{AB^2 + BC^2} = \sqrt{12^2 + 12^2} = 16.97$, or approximately 17. Therefore, the run of the hip rafter is to the run of the common rafter as 17 is to 12. Accordingly, in laying out the cuts, use figure 17 on one side of the square and the given rise in *inches per foot* on the other side. This also holds true for top and bottom cuts of the valley rafter when the plate intercept $AB =$ the run BC of the common rafter.

The line of measurement for the length of a hip and valley rafter is along the middle of the back or top edge, as on common and jack rafters. The rise is the same as that of a common rafter, and the run of a hip rafter is the horizontal distance from the plumb line of its rise to the outside of the plate at the foot of the hip rafter, as shown in Fig. 28.

In applying the source for cuts of hip or valley rafters, *use the distance 17 on the body of the square in the same way as 12 was used for common rafters.* When the plate distance between hip and common rafters is equal to half the span or run of the common rafter, the line of run of the hip will lie at 45° to the line of the common rafter, as indicated in Fig. 27.

The length of a hip rafter, as given in the framing table on the square, is the distance from the ridge board to the outer edge of the plate. In practice, deduct from this length one-half the

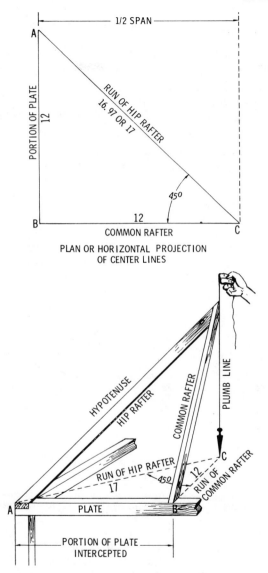

Fig. 27. View of hip and common rafters in respect to each other.

159

thickness of the ridge board, and add for any projection beyond the plate for the eave. Fig. 29A shows the correction for the table length of a hip rafter to allow for a ridge board, and Fig. 29B shows the correction at the plate end which may or may not be made as in Fig. 30.

The table length, as read from the square, must be reduced an amount equal to *MS*. This is equal to the hypotenuse (ab) of the little triangle abc, which in value $= \sqrt{ac^2 + bc^2} = \sqrt{ac^2 \times (\text{half thickness of ridge})^2}$. In ordinary practice, take *MS as equal to* half the thickness of the ridge. The plan and side view of

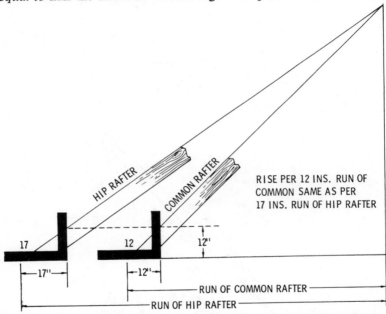

RISE PER 12 INS. RUN OF
COMMON SAME AS PER
17 INS. RUN OF HIP RAFTER

HIP RAFTER

COMMON RAFTER

17

12

12'

17"

12'

RUN OF COMMON RAFTER

RUN OF HIP RAFTER

Fig. 28. Hip and common rafters shown in the same plane, illustrating the use of 12 for the common rafter and 17 for the hip rafter.

the hip rafter shows the table length and the correction *MS*, which must be deducted from the table length so that the sides of the rafter at the end of the bottom cut will intersect the outside edges of the plate. The table length of the hip rafter, as read on the framing square, will cover the span from the ridge to the outside cover *a* of the plate, but the side edges of the hip intersect the plates at *b*

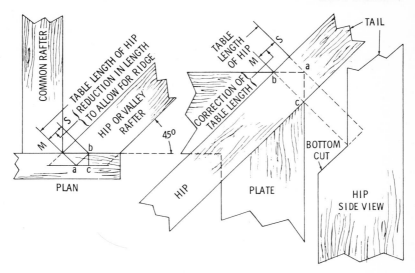

Fig. 29. *Correction in table for top cut to allow for half thickness of ridge board.*

and *c*. The distance that *a* projects beyond a line connecting *bc* or *MS,* must be deducted; that is, measured backward toward the ridge end of the hip. In making the bottom cut of a valley rafter, it should be noted that a valley rafter differs from a hip rafter in that the correction distance for the table length must be added instead of subtracted, as for a hip rafter. A distance *MS* was subtracted from the table length of the hip rafter in Fig. 29B, and an equal distance (*LF*) was added for the valley rafter in Fig. 30.

After the plumb cut is made, the end must be mitered outward for a hip, as in Fig. 31, and inward for a valley, as in Fig. 32, to receive the *fascia*. A *fascia* is the narrow vertical member fastened to the outside ends of the rafter tails. The miter cuts are shown with full tails in Fig. 33, which illustrates hip and valley rafters in place on the plate.

Side Cuts of Hip and Valley Rafters

These rafters have a side or cheek cut at the ridge end. In the absence of a framing square, a simple method of laying out the side cut for a 45° hip or valley rafter is as follows:

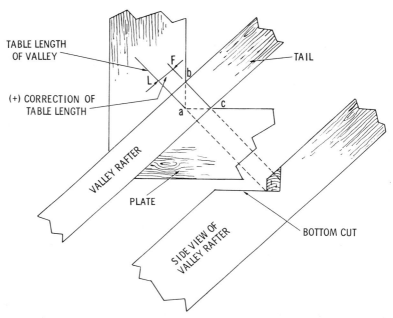

Fig. 30. Side view of valley rafter showing bottom and seat cut at top plate.

Measure back on the edge of the rafter from point *A* of the top cut, as shown in Fig. 34. Distance *AC* is equal to the thickness of the rafter. Square across from *C* to *B* on the opposite edge, and scribe line *AB,* which gives the side cut. *FA* is the top cut, and *AB* is the side cut. Here *A*, the point from which half the thickness of the rafter is measured, is seen at the top end of the cut.

This rule does not hold for any angle other than 45°.

BACKING OF HIP RAFTERS

By definition, the term *backing* is the bevel upon the top side of a hip rafter which allows the roofing boards to fit the top of the rafter without leaving a triangular hole between it and the back of the roof covering. The height of the hip rafter, measured on the outside surface vertically upward from the outside corner

162

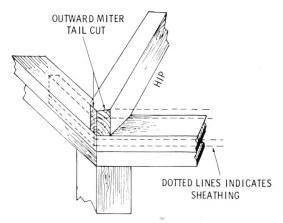

Fig. 31. Flush hip rafter miter cut.

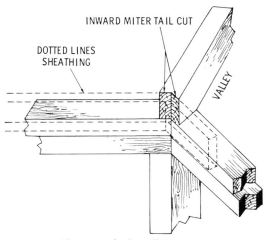

Fig. 32. Flush valley miter cut.

of the plate, will be the *same as that of the common rafter measured from the same line,* whether the hip is backed or not. This is not true for an unbacked valley rafter when the measurement is made at the center of the timber.

The graphical method of finding the backing of hip rafters is shown in Fig. 35. Let *AB* be the span of the building, and *OD* and *OC* the plan of two unequal hips. Lay off the given rise as shown.

163

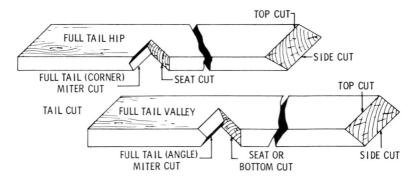

Fig. 33. Full tail hip and valley rafters showing all cuts.

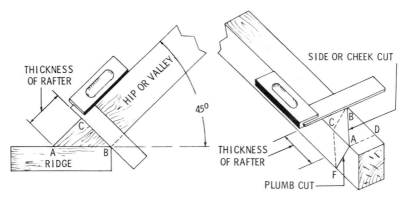

Fig. 34. A method of obtaining a side cut of 45° hip or valley rafter without aid of a framing table.

Then *DE* and *CF* are the lengths of the two unequal hips. Take any point, such as *G* on *DE*, and erect a perpendicular cutting *DF* at *H*. Revolve *GH* to *J*, that is, make *HJ = GH*, draw *NO* perpendicular to *OD* and through *H*. Join *J* to *N* and *O*, giving a bevel angle *NJO,* which is the backing for rafter *DE*. Similarly, the bevel angle *NJO* is found for the backing of rafter *CF*.

JACK RAFTERS

As outlined in the classification, there are several kinds of jack rafters as distinguished by their relation with other rafters of the roof. These various jack rafters are known as:

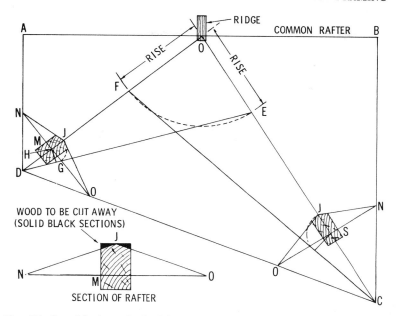

Fig. 35. Graphical method of finding length of rafters and backing of hip rafters.

1. Hip jacks.
2. Valley jacks.
3. Cripple jacks.

The distinction between these three kinds of jack rafters, as shown in Fig. 36, is as follows: *Rafters which are framed between a hip rafter and the plate are hip jacks; those framed between the ridge and a valley rafter are valley jacks; those framed between hip and valley rafters are cripple jacks.*

The term cripple is applied because the ends or *feet* of the rafters are cut off—the rafter does not extend the full length from ridge to plate. From this point of view, a valley jack is sometime erroneously called cripple; it is virtually a semi-cripple rafter, but confusion is avoided by using the term cripple for rafters framed between the hip and valley rafters, as above defined.

Jack rafters are virtually *discontinuous common rafters.* They are cut off by the intersection of a hip or valley, or both, before

165

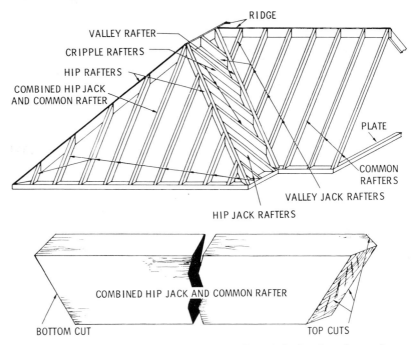

Fig. 36. A perspective view of hip and valley roof showing the various kinds of jack rafters, and enlarged detail of combined hip jack and common rafters showing cuts.

reaching the full length from plate to ridge. Their lengths are found in the same way as for common rafters—the number 12 being used on one side of the square and the rise in inches per foot run on the other side. This gives the length of jack rafter per foot run, and is true for all jacks—hip, valley, and cripple.

In actual practice, carpenters usually measure the length of hip or valley jacks from the long point to the ridge, instead of along the center of the top, no reduction being made for one-half the diagonal thickness of the hip or valley rafter. Cripples are measured from long point to long point, no reduction being made for the thickness of the hip or valley rafter.

As no two jacks are of the same length, various methods of procedure are employed in framing, as:

1. Beginning with shortest jack.
2. Beginning with longest jack.
3. Using framing table.

Shortest Jack Method

Begin by finding the length of the shortest jack. Take its spacing from the corner, measured on the plates, which in the case of a 45° hip is equal to the jacks run. The length of this first jack will be the common difference which must be added to each jack to get the length of the next longer jack.

Longest Jack Method

Where the longest jack is a full-length rafter (that is, a common rafter), first find the length of the longest jack, then count the spaces between jacks and divide the length of the longest jack by number of spaces. The quotient will be the *common difference*. Then frame the longest jack and make each jack shorter than the preceding jack by this common difference.

Framing Table Method

On various steel squares, there are tables giving the length of the shortest jack rafters corresponding to the various spacings, such as 16, 20, and 24 in. between centers for the different pitches. This length is also the *common difference* and thus serves for obtaining the length of all the jacks.

Example—Find the length of the shortest jack or the *common difference* in the length of the jack rafters, where the rise of the roof is 10 inches per foot and the jack rafters are spaced 16 inches between centers; also, when spaced 20 inches between centers.

10 IN. RISE PER FT.

2|3	2|2	2|1	2|0	1|9		1|2	1|1	1|0
LENGTH OF MAIN RAFTERS PER FOOT RUN						16 95	16 28	15 62
" HIP OR VALLEY " " " "						78	20 22	19 70
DIFFERENCE IN LENGTH OF 16 INCHES CENTERS						25	21 704	20 83
" " " " 2 FEET "						94	32 56	31 24
SIDE CUT OF JACKS USE THE MARKS ∧ ∧ ∧ ∧							8⅞	9¼
" " HIP OR VALLEY " " ✳ ✳ ✳ ✳							10⅛	10⅜
2|2	2|1	2|0	1|9	1|8	1|7	1|0	9	8

LENGTH SHORTEST JACK 16 IN. CENTER

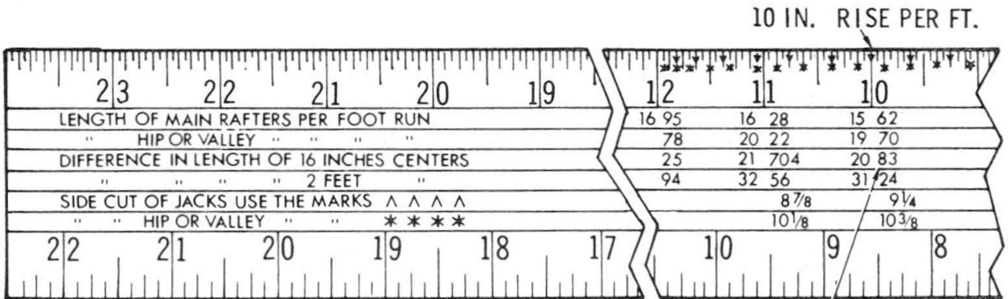

Fig. 37. Square showing table for shortest jack rafter at 16″ on center.

Fig. 37 shows the reading of the jack table on the square for 16-inch centers, and Fig. 38 shows the reading on the square for 20-inch centers.

Jack-Rafter Cuts

Jack rafters have top and bottom cuts which are laid out the same as for common rafters, and also side cuts which are laid out the same as for a hip rafter. To lay off the top or plumb cut with a square, take 12 on the tongue and the rise in inches (of common rafter) per foot run on the blade, and mark along the blade as in Fig. 39. The following example illustrates the use of the framing square in finding the side cut.

Example—Find the side cut of a jack rafter framed to a 45° hip or valley for a rise of 8 inches per foot run. Fig. 40 shows the reading on the jack side-cut table of the framing square, and Fig. 41 shows the method of placing the square on the timber to obtain the side cut. It should be noted that different makers of squares use different setting numbers, but the ratios are always the 'same.

METHOD OF TANGENTS

The tangent value is made use of in determining the side cuts of jack, hip, or valley rafters. By taking a circle with a radius of

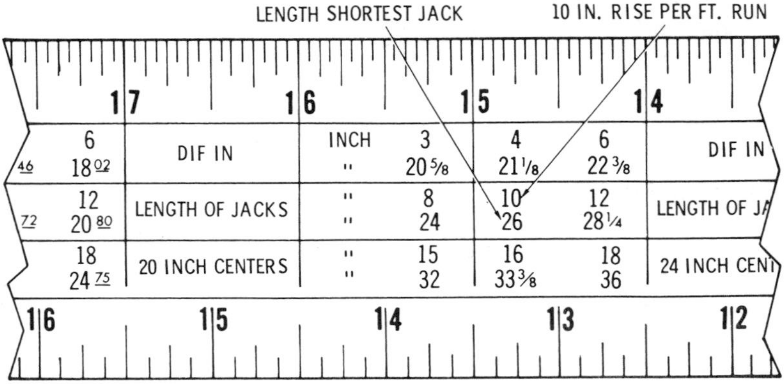

Fig. 38. *Square showing table for shortest jack rafter at 20" on center.*

168

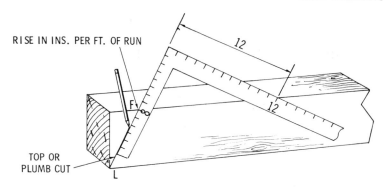

RISE IN INS. PER FT. OF RUN

TOP OR
PLUMB CUT

**Fig. 39. Method of finding plumb and side cuts of jack framed to 45°
hip or valley.**

12 inches, the value of the tangent can be obtained *in terms of
the constant of the common rafter run.*

Considering rafters with zero pitch, as shown in Fig. 42, if the
common rafter is 12 ft. long, the tangent *MS* of a 45° hip is the
same length. Placing the square on the hip, setting to 12 on the

JACK SIDE CUT   8 IN. RISE PER FT. RUN

			INCH				
4 25¼	6 26⅞	FIG'S GIVING	"	3 7¾ 8	4 99¼	6 9 10	FIG'S GIVIN
10 31¼	12 34	SIDE CUT	"	8 10 12	10 10 13	12 12 17	SIDE CUT OF HIP ON
16 40	12 43¼	OF JACKS	"	15 10 16	16 9 15	18 10 18	VALLEY RAFTER

**Fig. 40. A framing square showing readings for side cut of jack cor-
responding to 8-inch rise per foot run.**

tongue and 12 on the body will give the side cut at the ridge *when
there is no pitch* (at *M*) as in Fig. 43. Placing the square on the
jack with the same setting numbers (12, 12) as at *S*, will give the
face cut for the jack when framed to a 45° hip with zero pitch; that
is, when all of the timbers lie in the same plane.

169

OCTAGON RAFTERS

On an octagon or eight-sided roof, the rafters joining the corners are called octagon rafters, and are a little longer than the common

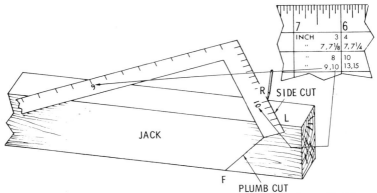

Fig. 41. Method of placing framing square on jack to lay off side cut for an 8-inch rise.

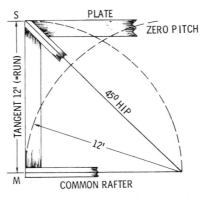

Fig. 42. A roof with zero pitch showing the common rafter and the tangent as being the same lengh.

rafter and shorter than the hip or valley rafters of a square building of the same span. The relation between the run of an octagon and a common rafter is shown in Fig. 44 as being as 13 is to 12. That is, for each foot run of a common rafter, an octagon rafter would have a run of 13 inches. Hence, to lay off the top or bottom cut of an octagon rafter, *place the square on the timber with the*

170

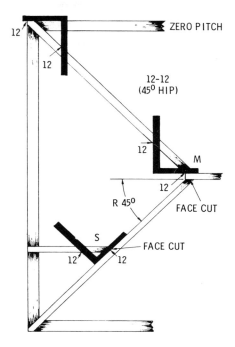

**Fig. 43. Zero pitch square 45° roof showing applica-
tion of the framing square to give side cuts at ridge.**

*13 on the tongue and the rise of the common rafter per foot run
on the blade,* as shown graphically in Fig. 45. The method of laying
out the top and bottom cut with the 13 rise setting is shown in
Fig. 46.

The length of an octagon rafter may be obtained by scaling the
diagonal on the square for 13 on the tongue and the rise in inches
per foot run of a common rafter, and multiplying by the number
of feet run of a common rafter. The principle involved in determining the amount of backing of an octagon rafter (or any other
polygon) is the same as for hip rafters. The backing is determined
by *the tangent of the angle whose adjacent side is 1/2 the rafter
thickness and whose angle is equivalent to one-half the central
angle.*

171

PREFABRICATED ROOFS

Definite savings in material and labor requirements through the use of preassembled wood roof trusses make truss framing an effective means of cost reduction in small dwelling construction. In a 26′ × 32′ dwelling, the use of trusses can result in a substantial cost saving and a reduction in use of lumber of almost 30% as compared with conventional rafter and joist construction. In addition to cost savings, roof trusses offer other advantages of increased flexibility for interior planning, and added speed and efficiency in site erection procedures.

For many years, trusses have been used extensively in commercial and industrial buildings, and are very familiar in bridge construction. In the case of small residential structures, truss construction in the past has been the exception rather than the rule, largely because small-house building has not had the benefit of careful detailing and engineered design that would permit the most efficient use of materials.

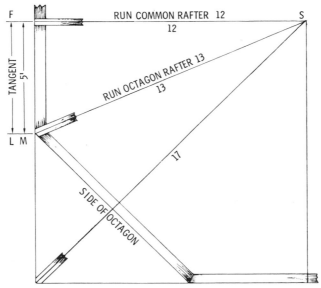

Fig. 44. Details of an octagon roof showing relation in length between common and octagon rafters.

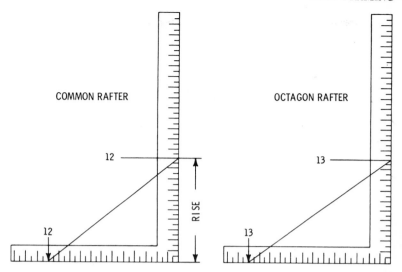

Fig. 45. Diagram showing that for equal rise, the run of octagon rafters is 13-inches, to 12-inches for the common rafters.

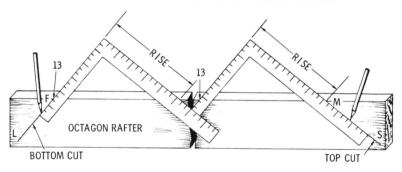

Fig. 46. Method of laying off bottom and top cuts of an octagon rafter with a square using the 13 rise setting.

During the last several years, however, special efforts have been made to apply engineering design to small houses. One of the results has been the development of light wood trusses which permit substantial savings in the case of lumber. Not only may the framing lumber be smaller in dimension than in conventional framing, but trusses may also be spaced 24 inches on center as

173

compared to the usual 16-inch spacing of rafter and joist construction.

The following figures show percentage savings in the 26′ × 32′ house through the use of trusses 24 inches on center:

Lumber Requirements for Trusses

28.4% less than for conventional framing at 16-inch spacing.

Labor Requirements for Trusses

36.8% less hours than for conventional framing at 16-inch spacing.

Total Cost of Trusses

29.1% less than conventional framing at 16-inch spacing.

The trusses consisted of 2 × 4 lumber at top and bottom chords, 1 × 6 braces, and double 1 × 6's for struts, with plywood gussets and splices, as shown in Fig. 47. The clear span of truss construction permits use of nonbearing partitions so that it is possible to eliminate the extra top plate required for bearing partitions used with conventional framing. It also permits a smaller floor girder to be used for floor construction since the floor does not have to support the bearing partition and help carry the roof load.

Aside from direct benefits of reduced cost and savings in material and labor requirements, roof trusses offer special advantages in helping to speed up site erection and overcome delays due to

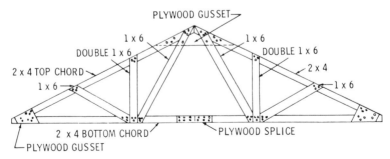

Fig. 47. Wood roof truss for small dwellings.

weather conditions. These advantages are reflected not only in improved construction methods, but also in further reductions in cost. With preassembled trusses, a roof can be put over the job quickly to provide protection against the weather.

Laboratory tests and field experience show that properly designed roof trusses are definitely acceptable for dwelling construction. The type of truss shown in Fig. 47 is suitable for heavy roofing and plaster ceiling finish. In assembling wood trusses, special care should be taken to achieve adequate nailing since the strength of trusses is, to a large extent, dependent on the fastness of the connection between members. Care should also be exercised in selecting materials for trusses. Lumber equal in stress value to No. 2 dimension shortleaf southern pine is suitable; any lower quality is not recommended.

ROOF VENTILATION

Adequate ventilation is necessary in preventing condensation in buildings. Condensation may occur in the walls, in the crawl space under the structure, in basements, on windows, etc. Condensation is most likely to occur in structures during cold weather when interior humidity is high. Proper ventilation under the roof allows moisture-laden air to escape during the winter heating season, and also allows the hot dry air to escape during the winter heating season. It also allows the hot dry air of the summer season to escape which will keep the house cooler. The upper areas of a structure are usually ventilated by the use of louvers or ventilators. The various types of ventilators used are as follows:

1. Roof louvers (Fig. 48).

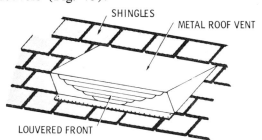

Fig. 48. Illustrating a typical roof ventilator.

175

2. Cornice ventilators (Fig. 49).

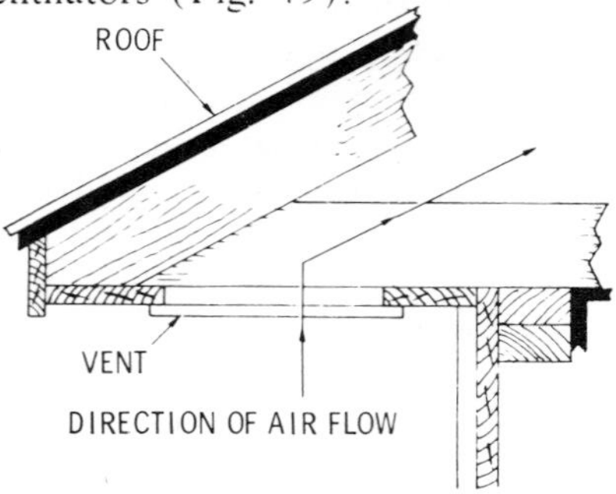

Fig. 49. Illustrating a cornice ventilator.

3. Gable louvers (Fig. 50).

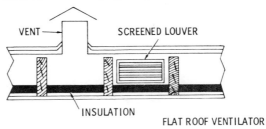

Fig. 50. A typical gable ventilator.

4. Flat-roof ventilators (Fig. 51).

Fig. 51. Illustrating a typical flat roof vent.

5. Crawl-space ventilators (Fig. 52).

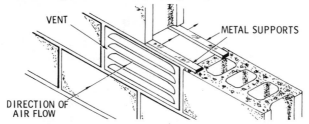

Fig. 52. A typical crawl space ventilator.

6. Ridge ventilators (Fig. 53).

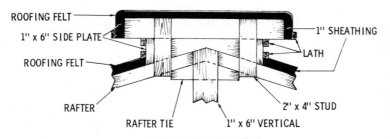

RIDGE VENTILATOR DETAIL

Fig. 53. A ridge type ventilator.

The upper structure ventilator, one of the most common methods of ventilating, is by the use of wood or metal louver frames. There are many types, sizes, and shapes of louvers. The following points should be considered when building or installing the various ventilators.

1. The size and number of ventilators is determined by the size of the area to be ventilated.
2. The minimum net open area should be 1/4 square inch for every square foot of ceiling area.
3. Most louver frames are usually 5 inches wide.
4. The back edge should be rabbeted out for a screen or door, or both.
5. Three-quarter inch slots are used and spaced about 1 3/4 inches apart.
6. Sufficient slant or slope to the slots should be provided to prevent rain from driving in.

177

7. For best operation, upper structure louvers are placed as near the top of the gable roof as possible.

The crawl-space installed in foundation structures should be well ventilated. Air circulation under the floor prevents excessive condensation, which causes warping, swelling, twisting and rotting of the lumber. These vents are usually called *foundation louvers,* some types are used for crawl spaces if ever needed. They are set in the foundation as it is being built. A good foundation vent should be equipped with a copper or bronze screen and adjustable shutters for opening and closing of the louvers. The size of the vents should be figured on the same basis as that used for upper structure ventilation.

SUMMARY

The primary object of a roof in any climate is to keep out the rain and the cold. There are numerous forms of roofs and an endless variety of shapes. The frame of most roofs is made up of timbers called rafters. The terms used in connection with roofs are span, total rise, total run, unit of run, rise in inches, pitch, cut of roof, line length, and plumb and level lines.

Rafters are the supports for the roof covering and serve in the same manner as do joists for floors or do studs for the walls. Rafters are constructed from ordinary 2 × 6, 2 × 8, or 2 × 10 lumber, spaced 16 to 24 inches on center. Various kinds of rafters used in roof construction are common, hip, valley, jack, and octagon. The length of a rafter may be found in several ways—by calculation, with a steel framing square, or with the aid of a framing table.

Definite savings in material and labor through the use of preassembled wood roof trusses make truss framing an effective means of cost reduction in small buildings. In addition to cost savings, roof trusses offer other advantages of increased flexibility for interior planning, and added speed and efficiency in site erection procedures.

During the last several years, engineering designs have resulted in development of light wood trusses which permit substantial savings because they may be spaced 24 inches on center as compared to the usual 16-inch spacing. Aside from the direct benefits of reduced cost and savings in material and labor requirements, roof trusses offer special advantages in interior design, since the roof span can be increased without center supports. This offers unlimited advantages in floor areas for auditoriums and meeting rooms.

REVIEW QUESTIONS

1. Name the various kinds of rafters used in roof construction.
2. Name the various terms used in connection with roofs.
3. What is preassembled truss roofing? What are some advantages in this type of construction?
4. Why is adequate roof and crawl-space ventilation needed?
5. What are jack rafters and octagon rafters?

CHAPTER 11

Skylights

A skylight is any window placed in the roof of a building or ceiling of a room for the admission of light and/or ventilation. Skylights are very essential to lighting and ventilating top floors and factories where the roofs are flat and where there is not much side lighting.

Fig. 1 shows a simple hinged skylight and detail of the hinge. The skylight may be operated from below by the control device, having an adjustment eye in the support for securing the hinged sash at various degrees of opening. A skylight is often placed at the top of a flight of stairs leading to the roof, the projecting structure having framed in it the skylight and a doorway, as in Fig. 2.

Where fireproof construction is required, skylights are made of metal. Side-pivoted sash are shown in Fig. 3, a type desirable for engine and boiler rooms where a great amount of steam and heat is generated, and where a storm coming through them would do little harm if thoughtlessly left open. The sash may be operated separately by pulleys, or all on one adjuster. The ends may be stationary.

Wire glass should be used for skylights so that, if broken, it will not fall and possibly injure someone below. Wire glass is cast with the wire netting running through its center and is manufactured in many styles and sizes. Fig. 4 shows two forms of wire glass. The approved method of fastening the glass is by retaining bars which are used instead of putty.

Skylights are becoming very popular in residential dwellings, especially those with cathedral-type ceilings. The skylights are generally a luxury item, and the additional cost should be considered.

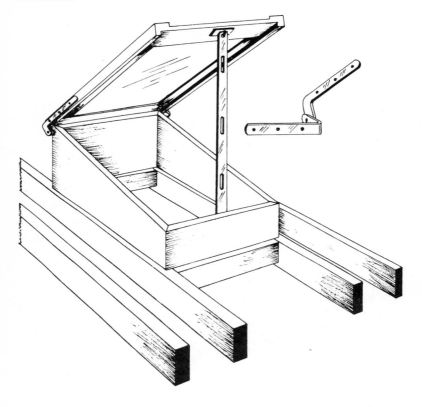

Fig. 1. Hinged skylight framed into roof.

They are generally stationary and made of glass or corrugated translucent panels which come in several different colors, and are set in waterproof frames which are permanently installed and sealed in the roof.

A skylight is often used in an inside room where there are no windows in the walls for natural light or ventilation. In the deep southern part of the United States where the sun is hot and penetrating, skylights are used for heating rooms. In some cases, the sun is used to heat water stored in ceiling tanks.

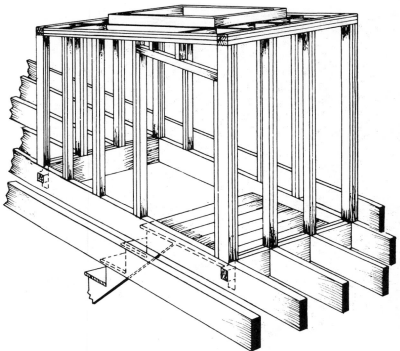

Fig. 2. View of entrance to roof, or projection framework containing framed opening for skylight and doorway.

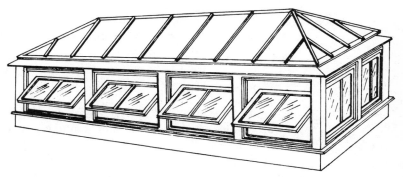

Fig. 3. Metal fireproof ventilating skylight.

183

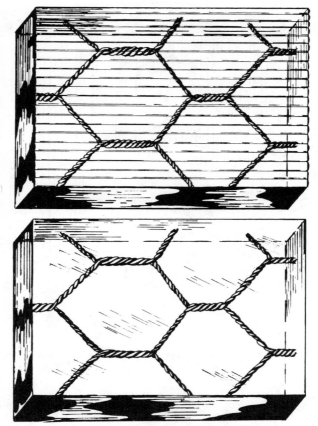

Fig. 4. Typical forms of wire reinforced glass.

SUMMARY

Skylights are becoming very popular in residential dwellings. A skylight is generally a luxury item, and the additional cost should be considered. In most cases, they are stationary and made of glass or corrugated translucent material. Glass with wire netting cast through the center is generally used so that, if broken, it will not fall and injure someone below.

A skylight is often placed at the top of a flight of stairs leading to the roof, or in an inside room where no side windows are available. They may also be used in areas where the sun penetrates the glass for heating rooms. In some cases, the sun is used to heat water stored in ceiling tanks.

REVIEW QUESTIONS

1. What are some of the advantages of a skylight?
2. What type of glass is best to use in a skylight?
3. Why are skylights used in some dwellings?

CHAPTER 12

Porches and Patios

The terms, stoop, porch, and veranda are usually applied without distinction to mean a *covered structure forming an outside entrance to a building.*

TYPES OF CONSTRUCTION

A distinction should be made between these terms and the word *stoop* which means *an uncovered platform at the door of a house, usually having steps with a hand rail at each side. A stoop is virtually a primitive porch without a cover.*

Porches—Wooden porch floors are a thing of the past. Unless the wood is pressure treated with creosote or penetrating oils, it will soon decay and need replacing. Concrete floors built on top of a good solid foundation, or a slab poured on top of the ground, is being used today. The porch may or may not have a roof, which will depend upon the building design. This does not pose a problems since awnings are available to give the home owner maximum use of his porch floor.

Patio—This type of construction is often done after the house or dwelling has been completed. A patio constructed in the right place and designed properly can not only make your home the most outstanding house in the neighborhood, but can give your family hours of pleasant outdoor living. The foundation for a patio floor should be well constructed to eliminate any cracking due to settlement. Since there will be little if any weight on the floor, the foundation will not have to be built below the frost line.

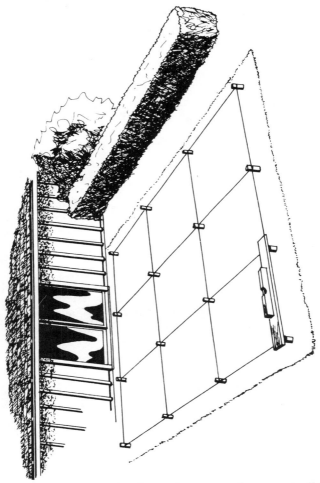

Fig. 1. Staking out and leveling a large area for concrete slab.

Laying a Patio Floor—As always, the first stage is to decide on the boundaries of the area and to mark them out with stakes and string. If the paved area is to be large, it should be divided into smaller sections and leveled, as shown in Fig. 1.

The stakes are driven into the ground until the tops are level in both directions. This is checked by a level placed on a straight-

Fig. 2. Illustrating a typical patio wall.

edge across the stakes. The form boards are then nailed to and even with the tops of the outer stakes.

An interesting and attractive effect can be obtained by adding a design to your patio floor. Adding color to the concrete, and different finishing techniques to the floor are just a few ideas. Brick or flagstone are also two very popular materials often used for a patio floor.

Building a Small Patio Wall—Small patio walls provide an attractive informal appearance that can easily be maintained. There are a number of occasions when a low wall can provide the answer

189

to the problem of privacy. Constructing such a wall is not a job that an amateur should be afraid of tackling. It is possible to purchase several types of precast block or brick which have an informal appearance suitable for a patio, as shown in Fig. 2.

Depending on the circumstances, a wall can be single thickness, with or without a flat capping on top, or it can be a double thickness wall joined at the ends which can be filled with earth. These double walls should be at least three inches in thickness with a four-inch cavity. Up to the height of two feet, the wall will not need to be tied together. Alternatively, the wall can be single thickness with hollow piers at the ends forming a flower box or lamp post.

Wrought-iron railings and columns which are strong, yet quick and easy to install, can be used for your patio. Railings are an attractive and economical way to add charm and beauty to your patio. Adjustable railing can be purchased in many designs and shapes to fit any contour or floor plan.

SUMMARY

Porches and patios are often constructed after the house or dwelling has been completed. A patio constructed in the right place and designed properly can make your home the most attractive house in the neighborhood.

First, decide on the area and mark the boundaries with stakes and string. Many interesting and attractive effects can be obtained by adding a design to your patio floor. Adding color to the concrete, or different finishes or designs, are just a few ideas. Two very popular materials often used for patio or porch floors are brick or flagstone. Interesting and attractive designs can be obtained when using such material.

Many times a small patio wall or fence will provide an attractive informal appearance that can easily be maintained. The wall can be constructed with brick or concrete blocks in many attractive designs. In many cases, wrought-iron railings can be installed.

This type of railing is quick and easy to install and can add charm and beauty to your patio.

REVIEW QUESTIONS

1. Why are wooden porch floors a thing of the past?
2. Why are patio floors generally constructed above the frost line?
3. What type of patio wall is generally constructed?

CHAPTER 13

Chimneys and Fireplaces

Chimneys and fireplaces are not usually constructed by the carpenter, although many tradesmen are adept at more than one skill. To the general builder, contractor, architect, and prospective home owner, the construction features of these masonry units are of interest.

CHIMNEYS

The proper construction of a chimney is more complicated than the average person realizes. Not only must it be mechanically strong, it must also be pleasing to the eye and correctly designed to provide a proper draft. A chimney can be too large as well as too small.

Conditions for Proper Draft

The power that produces a natural draft in a chimney is due to the small difference in weight between the hot gases in the flue and the colder air outside. The hot gases are lighter and will therefore rise, providing a natural draft in the chimney.

A frequent cause of poor draft, is that the peak of the roof extends higher than the top of the chimney. This will cause downdrafts as the wind sweeps across the roof and swirls down on top of the chimney. To prevent this condition, make sure the top of the chimney is at least 2 feet above the peak of the roof, as in Fig. 1A. The height above a flat roof should not be less than 3 feet, as in Fig. 1B.

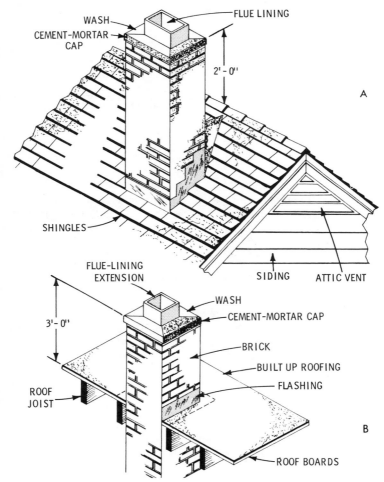

Fig. 1. Chimney heights; (A) Above a gable roof (B) Above a flat roof.

Another cause of poor draft is restrictions of some sort inside the chimney that offer a resistance to the free flow of gases. This restriction may be in the form of an offset that is too abrupt. Therefore, chimneys should be built with as little offset as possible. This not only provides a better draft, but prevents the accumula-

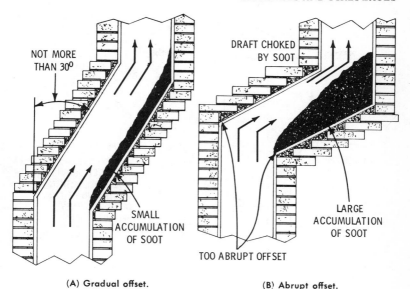

NOT MORE
THAN 30°

SMALL
ACCUMULATION
OF SOOT

DRAFT CHOKED
BY SOOT

LARGE
ACCUMULATION
OF SOOT

TOO ABRUPT OFFSET

(A) Gradual offset.   (B) Abrupt offset.

Fig. 2. An offset in a flue must not be too abrupt.

tion of soot and ashes that may eventually block the chimney completely. Fig. 2 shows the effect of a gradual offset and the effect of an abrupt offset. Neither of these chimneys illustrate good design, however, because the offset should never be displaced so much that the center of gravity of the upper portion falls outside the area of the lower portion (Fig. 3). Otherwise, the unit will not be structurally sound and may develop cracks, or in extreme cases, fall.

Foundations

When consideration is given to the amount of weight contained in even the smallest chimney, it becomes evident that a good foundation is necessary to support it properly. In no case should the foundation be less than 18 inches deep. If the chimney is built on an outside wall, the foundation must extend to below the frost line. This depth varies in different localities, being as much as 48 inches in some northern sections of the United States.

195

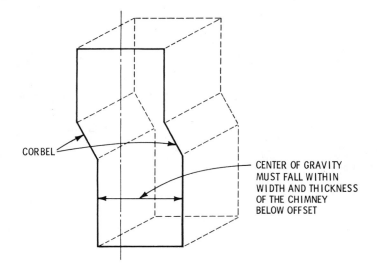

CORBEL

CENTER OF GRAVITY
MUST FALL WITHIN
WIDTH AND THICKNESS
OF THE CHIMNEY
BELOW OFFSET

Fig. 3. The offset (corbel) of a chimney must be kept within certain limits.

The foundation should extend at least 6 inches on all sides of the chimney and should be of reinforced concrete for larger fireplace units. The foundations for smaller chimneys do not necessarily need this reinforcement.

Construction

A straight flue is the most efficient and easiest to build. If an offset is necessary, it should not be displaced by more than the amount shown in Fig. 3, and should form an angle of less than 30° with the vertical.

Common brick is the most widely used material in the construction of chimneys. When this type brick is laid in a single course, the wall of the unit will be 4 inches thick and should be lined with a fire-clay flue lining. *Never omit the lining or replace it with plaster.* The normal expansion and contraction of the walls will cause a plaster lining to crack, forming an opening to the outside of the chimney wall. This will result in a definite fire hazard. If a flue liner is not used, the wall should be no less than 8 inches thick, with the mortar joints carefully pointed. The plaster is applied to the inside of the flue as it is built. A bag filled with shavings may be placed in the flue and drawn up as the work progresses. If this bag fits the flue snugly, it will catch

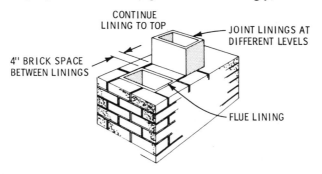

CONTINUE
LINING TO TOP

JOINT LININGS AT
DIFFERENT LEVELS

4" BRICK SPACE
BETWEEN LININGS

FLUE LINING

Fig. 4. Flue liners should extend to the top of the chimney and project about 4 inches. When two or more flues are present, they should be separated by 4" of brick, and the joints of the liners should be staggered so they do not occur at the same level.

all the plaster droppings and will remove any mortar projecting into the opening. The use of a bag in this manner is also recommended when a flue liner is used, especially if there is an offset in the chimney.

The flue lining should extend the entire height of the chimney, projecting about 4 inches above the cap, as in Fig. 4. A slope should then be formed of cement to within 2 inches of the top of the lining. This gives an upward direction to the wind currents

Table 1. Rectangular and Round Flue Linings

| Rectangular flues | | Round flues | |
outside dimensions (inches)	net inside area (square inches)	inside diameter (inches)	net inside area (square inches)
4½ X 8½		6	28.3
4½ X 13		7	38.5
4½ X 18		8	50.3
8½ X 8½	52	9	63.6
8½ X 13	80	10	78.5
8½ X 18		12	113.
13 X 13	126	15	176.7
13 X 18	169	18	254.5
18 X 18	240	20	314.2
		24	452.4

across the top of the flue and tends to prevent rain and snow being blown in. For chimneys having more than one flue, at least a 4-inch course of brick must separate the liners. These liners come in various dimensions. Table 1 shows the sizes generally available. The length of each unit is normally 24 inches, although lengths from 20 to 30 inches are sometimes available.

FIREPLACES

Fireplaces are being included in nearly every medium-priced and luxury home now being built. While many such units are mainly ornamental, the cheerful and cozy feeling that a crackling blaze in a fireplace can give cannot be duplicated by any other heating method. Fireplaces are considered appropriate in a living room, dining room, and bedroom. Many modern house

Table 2. Recommended Dimension for Fireplaces

Opening Width (inches)	Opening Height (inches)	Depth (inches)	Minimum back wall (horizontal) (inches)	Vertical back wall (inches)	Inclined back wall (inches)	Outside dimensions of standard rectangular flue lining (inches)	Inside diameter of standard round flue lining (inches)
24	24	16-18	14	14	16	8½ X 8½	10
28	24	16-18	14	14	16	8½ X 8½	10
24	28	16-18	14	14	20	8½ X 8½	10
30	28	16-18	16	14	20	8½ X 13	10
36	28	16-18	22	14	20	8½ X 13	12
42	28	16-18	28	14	20	8½ X 18	12
36	32	18-20	20	14	24	8½ X 18	12
42	32	18-20	26	14	24	13 X 13	12
48	32	18-20	32	14	24	13 X 13	15
42	36	18-20	26	14	28	13 X 13	15
48	36	18-20	32	14	28	13 X 18	15
54	36	18-20	38	14	28	13 X 18	15
60	36	18-20	44	14	28	13 X 18	15
42	40	20-22	24	17	29	13 X 13	15
48	40	20-22	30	17	29	13 X 18	15
54	40	20-22	36	17	29	13 X 18	15
60	40	20-22	42	17	29	18 X 18	18
66	40	20-22	48	17	29	18 X 18	18
72	40	22-28	51	17	29	18 X 18	18

plans are even including them in the kitchen, basement, and patio porch.

All fireplaces should be built in accordance with a few simple essentials of correct design if they are to perform satisfactorily. Their size should match the room in which they are to be used, both from the standpoint of appearance and operation. If the fireplace is too small, it will not adequately heat the room—if too large, a fire that fills the combustion chamber will be much too hot for the room and will waste fuel.

The location of the chimney usually determines the location of the fireplace, and is too often governed by structural considerations only. A fireplace should be located to provide a reasonable amount of seclusion and should not, therefore, be near doors that carry traffic from one part of the house to another.

Fireplace Design

In designing a fireplace, the type of fuel to be burned should be considered. In addition, the design should harmonize with the room in both proportion and detail. In the days of the early settlers of our land, wood was plentiful and fireplaces with openings as large as 7 feet wide and 5 feet high were common. These were often used for cooking as well as heating. Needless to say, they consumed huge amounts of fuel and were more likely to be smoky than not.

Where cordwood (4 ft. long) is readily available, a 30-inch wide opening is desirable for a fireplace. The wood is cut in half to provide pieces 24 inches long. If coal is to be burned, however, the opening can be narrower. Thirty inches is a practical height for any fireplace having an opening less than 6 feet wide. It will be found that, in general, the higher the opening, the greater is the chance the fireplace will smoke.

Another dimension to consider is the depth of the combustion chamber. Again, in general, the wider the opening the deeper the chamber should be. A shallow opening will provide more heat than a deep one of the same width, but will accommodate a smaller amount of fuel. Thus, a choice must be made as to which is the most important—a greater depth which permits the use of larger logs that burn longer or a shallow depth which takes smaller pieces of wood but provides more heat.

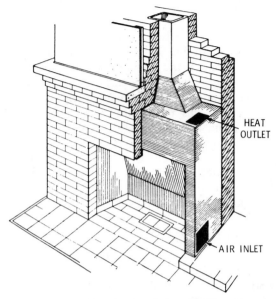

Fig. 5. A metal fireplace unit practically assures a smokeless fireplace.

In small fireplaces, a depth of 12 inches will provide adequate draft if the throat is constructed properly, but a minimum depth of 16 to 18 inches is advisable to lessen the danger of burning fuel falling out on the floor. *Screens of suitable design should be placed in front of all fireplaces.*

A fireplace 30 to 36 inches wide is usually suitable for a room having 300 square feet of floor area. The width should be increased for larger rooms, with all other dimensions being changed to correspond to the sizes listed in Table 2. Following these dimensions will result in a fireplace that operates correctly.

Modified Fireplaces

Metal fireplace units are now available in many different sizes and are designed to be set in place and concealed by the brick or stone used to lay up the fireplace. Fig. 5 shows one of these units. With this type of fireplace, the warm air is circulated throughout the room by the action of the air inlets and outlets provided in the metal unit. Cool air is drawn into the inlets at the bottom of the unit and is heated by contact with the metal sides. This heated air rises and is discharged through the outlets at the top. The inlets and outlets are connected to registers that may be located at the front or ends of the fireplace, or even in another room.

One of the main advantages of this type of modified fireplace is that the firebox is correctly designed and proportioned, and has the throat damper, smoke shelf, and chamber already fabricated. All this provides a fool-proof form for the masonry and greatly reduces the risk of failure and practically assures a smokeless fireplace. It must be remembered, however, that even though the fireplace is built correctly, it will not operate properly if the chimney is inadequate.

Manufacturers of these metal fireplace units claim that the labor and materials saved will offset the cost of the unit and that the saving in fuel will justify any net increase in first cost. A minimum life of 20 years is claimed for the type of units manufactured today.

The quantity and temperature of the heated air discharged from the registers in this type of fireplace will circulate heat into the coldest corners of a room and will deliver heated air through ducts to adjoining or overhead rooms, if desired. For example, heat could be diverted to a bathroom from a fireplace in the living room. The amount of heat delivered by some of the medium-size units is equivalent to that from 40 square feet of cast-iron radiators in a hot-water heating system. This is sufficient to heat a 15' x 18' room to 70°F when the outside temperature is 40°F. Additional heat can be obtained with some models by the use of circulation fans placed in the ductwork.

Fig. 6 shows another type of modified fireplace in which the circulated air is drawn in from outside through an air inlet *a*. The air is then heated as it rises through the back heating chamber *c* and tubes *t*, being discharged through register *b*. Combustion air is drawn into the fireplace opening *d*, and passes between the tubes and up the flue. Dampers are provided to close the air inlet and to regulate the amount of combustion air allowed to pass into the flue. Fig. 7 shows a cross-section of this type of modified fireplace.

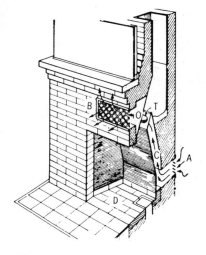

Fig. 6. A type of modified fireplace in which the air to be heated is drawn in from outside.

Prefabricated Fireplaces

Prefabricated fireplaces are now available in many designs and price ranges. These units fill the need for a low-cost fireplace that eliminates expensive masonry construction. This type of fireplace can be free-standing, mounted flush with the wall, or recessed into it, depending on the style selected. The unit shown in Fig. 7 has a cantilever designed hearth 15 inches above floor level and can burn wood up to 27 inches long. The outer shell is steel with stainless steel trim, while the firebox is formed of high-impact ceramic material.

The complete unit (except for the trim) is prime coated and ready to be painted with any interior paint to harmonize with the decorating scheme of the room. A flexible hearth screen is provided to prevent sparks from flying out of the firebox into the room.

Fireplace Construction

Fireplace construction is an exacting art. Preformed metal units may be used or the complete fireplace can be built of masonry materials. Fig. 9 shows the details of a typical fireplace. This, along with the following essentials, should prove helpful in the design and construction of any type of fireplace.

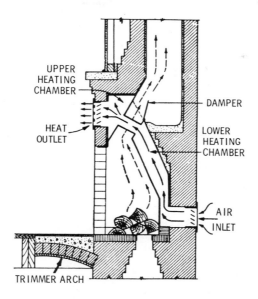

Fig. 7. A cross-sectional view of the modified fireplace shown in Fig. 6.

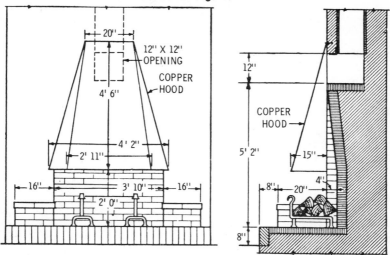

Fig. 8. A prefabricated type of fireplace that requires a minimum of masonry.

203

1. The flue must have sufficient cross-sectional area.
2. The throat must be constructed correctly and have a suitable damper.
3. The chimney must be high enough to provide a good draft.
4. The shape of the firebox must be such as to direct a maximum amount of radiated heat into the room.
5. A properly constructed smoke chamber must be provided.

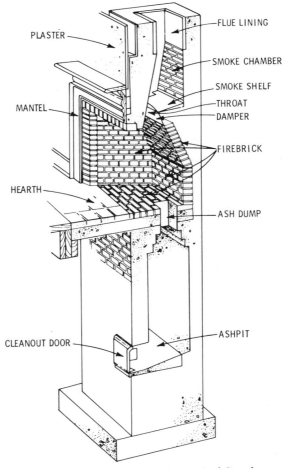

Fig. 9. Construction details of a typical fireplace.

Dimensions—Table 2 lists the recommended dimensions for fireplaces of various widths and heights. If a damper is installed, the width of the opening will depend on the width of the damper frame and slope of the back wall.

The width of the throat is determined by the opening of the hinged damper cover. The full damper opening should never be less than the cross-sectional area of the flue. When no damper is used, the throat opening should be 4 inches for fireplace not exceeding 4 feet in height.

Hearths—The hearth in conventional fireplaces should be flush with the floor to permit sweepings to be brushed into the fireplace opening. If a basement is located below the fireplace, an ash dump on the hearth near the back of the firebox is convenient. This dump consists of a metal frame about 5″ x 8″ with a pivoted plate through which the ashes can be dropped into a pit below.

With wooden floors, the hearth in front of the fireplace should be supported by masonry trimmer arches or other fire-resistant material, as shown in Figs. 7 and 9. The hearth should project at least 16 inches from the fireplace breast and should be constructed of brick, stone, terra cotta, reinforced concrete, or other fire-proof material at least 4 inches thick. The length of the hearth should not be less than the width of the fireplace opening plus 16 inches. The wooden centering under the trimmer arches may be removed after the mortar has set, although it may be left in place if desired.

Wall Thickness—Fireplace walls should never be less than 8 inches thick if of brick, or 12 inches thick if of stone. The back and sides of the firebox may be laid up with stone or hard-burned brick, although fire brick in fire clay is preferred. When firebricks are used, they should be laid flat with their long edges exposed to lessen the danger of their falling out. If they are placed on edge, however, metal ties should be built into the main brickwork to hold the firebrick in place.

Jambs—The jambs should be wide enough to give stability and a pleasing appearance to the fireplace, and are usually faced with ornamental brick, stone, or tile. When the fireplace opening is less than 3 feet wide, 12- or 16-inch jambs are usually sufficient, depending on whether a wood mantel is used or if the jambs are of exposed masonry. The edges of a wood mantel should be kept at least 8 inches away from the fireplace opening. Similar proportions of the jamb widths should be kept for wider openings and larger rooms.

Lintels—Lintels are used to support the masonry over the fireplace openings. These lintels may be 1/2" x 3" bars or 3 1/2" x 3 1/2" x 1/4" angle iron. Heavier lintels are required for wider openings.

If a masonry arch is used over the opening, the jambs should be heavy enough to resist the thrust imposed on them by the arch. Arches used over openings less than 4 feet wide seldom sag, but wider openings will cause trouble in this respect unless special construction techniques are employed.

Throats—The sides of the fireplace should be vertical up to the throat or damper opening, as shown in Fig. 10. The throat should be 6 or 8 inches or more above the bottom of the lintel and have an area that is not less than that of the flue. The width of the throat should be the same as the width of the fireplace opening. Starting 5 inches above the throat, the sides should be drawn in to equal the flue area.

Proper throat construction is necessary if the fireplace is to perform correctly, and the builder must make certain that the side walls are laid vertically until the throat has been passed and that the full length of opening is provided.

Smoke Shelf and Chamber—The smoke shelf is made by setting the brickwork back at the top of throat to the line of the flue wall for the full length of the throat. The depth of the shelf may vary from 6" to 12" or more, depending on the depth of the fireplace.

The smoke chamber is the space extending from the top of the throat up to the bottom of the flue proper, and between the side walls. The walls should be drawn inward at a 30° angle to the vertical after the top of the throat is passed. These walls should

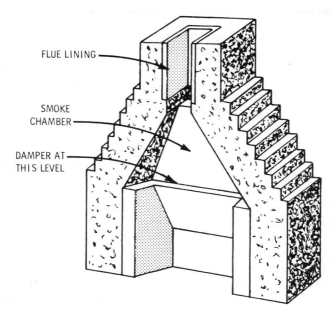

FLUE LINING

SMOKE CHAMBER

DAMPER AT THIS LEVEL

Fig. 10. View of the fireplace and flue opening.

be smoothly plastered with cement mortar not less than 1/2" thick.

Table 3. Sizes of Flue Linings for Various Size Fireplaces
(Based on a flue area equal to one-twelfth the fireplace opening)

Area of fireplace opening (square inches)	Outside dimensions of standard rectangular flue lining (inches)	Inside diameter of standard round flue lining (inches)
600	8½ X 8½	10
800	8½ X 13	10
1,000	8½ X 18	12
1,200	8½ X 18	12
1,400	13 X 13	12
1,600	13 X 13	15
1,800	13 X 18	15
2,000	13 X 18	15
2,200	13 X 18	15
2,400	18 X 18	18
2,600	18 X 18	18
2,800	18 X 18	18
3,000	18 X 18	18

Damper—A properly designed damper provides a means of regulating the draft and prevents excessive loss of heat from the room when the fireplace is not being used. A damper consists of a cast-iron frame with lid hinged so that the width of the throat opening may be varied from a completely closed to a wide-open position.

Regulating the opening with the damper prevents waste of heat up the chimney. Closing the damper in the summer keeps flies, mosquitos, and other insects from entering the house through the chimney. In houses heated by furnaces or other heating devices, lack of a fireplace damper may interfere with uniform heating of the house, whether or not there is a fire in the fireplace.

Flue—The area of lined flues should be at least $1/12$ the area of the fireplace opening, provided the chimney is at least 22 feet high, measured from the hearth. If the flue is shorter, or is unlined, its area should be at least $1/10$ the area of the fireplace opening. For example, a fireplace with an opening of 10 square feet (1440 square inches), needs a flue area of approximately 120 square inches if the chimney is 22' tall or 144 square inches if less than 22. The nearest commercial size of rectangular lining that would be suitable is the 13" x 13" size. A 15-inch round liner would also be suitable.

It is seldom possible to obtain a liner having the exact cross-sectional area required, but the inside area should never be less than that required. Always select the next larger size liner in such a case. Tables 1 or 3 can be used to select the proper size liner or for determining the size of fireplace opening for an existing flue. The area of the fireplace opening in square inches is obtained by multiplying the width by the height, both in inches.

SUMMARY

Proper construction of a chimney is more complicated than the average person realizes. A chimney can be too large as well as too small. Not only must it be mechanically strong, it must also be properly designed to provide the proper draft. A frequent cause of poor draft is that the peak of the roof extends higher than the top of the chimney.

A good foundation is necessary to support a properly built chimney. If a chimney is built on an outside wall, the foundation must extend well below the frost line. If a large fireplace is built in connection with the chimney, the foundation should extend at least 6 inches on all sides with reinforced concrete.

A straight flue is the most efficient design constructed. If an offset is necessary, it should not form an angle of more than 30 degrees. The most widely used material in chimney construction is brick or stone, and should never be designed without the use of a flue liner. The flue liner should always extend the entire height of the chimney and project about 4 inches above the chimney cap.

Fireplaces are becoming very popular in medium-priced and luxury homes now being built. All fireplaces should be built according to all rules and regulations to perform satisfactorily. Size should always match room area from the standpoint of appearance and operation.

REVIEW QUESTIONS

1. Why should chimneys always be built in a straight line?
2. How high should a chimney be built above the roof? Why?
3. Explain the purpose of the flue lining.
4. What should be considered when designing a fireplace?
5. Explain the purpose of the hearth, throat, and damper.

CHAPTER 14

Insulation of Buildings

It is probably true that, without further specification, the term *insulation* will be taken by most people to mean the material used as covering for electrical wiring. In the case of an electric wire, the insulation may be termed a barrier, as it prevents current from leaving the conductor. In the same sense, the insulation in a refrigerator is a barrier preventing the loss of heat to the air surrounding it.

The primary function of insulating a building is to provide a *barrier* against undesired temperature exchange. The insulation prevents the high outside temperature from entering the house during the *summer time,* and prevents the inside higher temperature from leaving the building during the *winter time.*

HEAT TRANSFER TERMS

Insulation of a building is usually concerned with the problem of reducing the transfer of heat from one region to another. This is generally called *thermal insulation.* There are three general methods by which this transfer can be accomplished. They are respectively called:

1. Conduction.
2. Convection.
3. Radiation.

The transfer of heat may be achieved by any one of the methods mentioned, or in combination, depending upon the particular conditions. In order to obtain a clear conception of the theoretical aspects involved, each one of the methods of heat transfer should be studied individually.

TRANSFER OF HEAT BY CONDUCTION

Conduction transfer of heat is a process which takes place in all solid materials. The amount of heat conduction from one region to another is proportional to the difference in temperature between the two regions in question. The ability to conduct heat varies widely among the various materials. Metals are in general much better conductors of heat than nonmetallic substances.

The numerical measure of the ability of a substance to conduct heat is called its *thermal conductivity*. This is customarily defined as the amount of heat in Btu's (British thermal units) which will flow in one hour through a uniform layer of material one square foot in area and one inch in thickness when the temperature difference between the surfaces of the layer is one degree Fahrenheit.

A Btu is the amount of heat necessary to raise the temperature of one pound of water 1°F., or more exactly, is equal to 1/180 part of the heat required to raise the temperature of one pound of water from 32° to 212°F. The insulating value or thermal *resistivity* of a material is equal to the reciprocal of its *conductivity*. Thermal conductivity is a property of the material itself, and does not depend upon the size and shape of the material in question; providing of course that the latter is of uniform structure.

It is therefore incorrect to speak of the conductivity of a wall or other structure, but it is correct to speak of the conductivity of the material or materials of which the structure is composed. With reference to the above, when dealing with a body such as a building wall, its insulating value as a whole is measured by a property known as conductance, and defined as the amount of heat flowing through the wall per unit time and per unit area, when the temperature difference between the surfaces of the wall is 1°F.

The insulating value or thermal resistance is equal to the *reciprocal* of the *conductance*. The conductance of a wall depends upon the conductivity, size, and arrangement of the materials of the wall. ·

If the wall, for example, consists of a single uniform material, its conductance is numerically equal to the conductivity of the

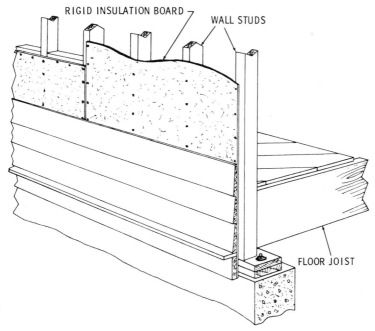

RIGID INSULATION BOARD

WALL STUDS

FLOOR JOIST

Fig. 1. The application of insulation board.

material divided by the thickness of the wall. Again, if the wall is composed of parallel layers of different materials, its conductance can be calculated from the respective thickness of the layers and the resistances of the materials used. Bear in mind that the insulating value of the wall is equal to the sum of the *resistances* of the different layers.

TRANSFER OF HEAT BY CONVECTION

In the transfer of heat in a liquid or a gas, the process is usually complicated by other factors besides conduction. In addition to

213

the ever present conduction, the heat transfer is greatly facilitated by the fluid motion called *convection*. This is set up either automatically, by reason of the temperature difference, or by means of mechanical stirring or blowing. The former is called *natural* or *free convection* and the latter *forced* or *induced convection*.

The air-movement in gravity-flow furnace pipes is caused by natural convection, as is the movement of steam from the boiler to the radiators in steam heating plants. Hot-water heating plants may depend upon natural convection to move the medium, or it may be *induced* by means of pumps.

TRANSFER OF HEAT BY RADIATION

A typical example of heat transfer of this kind is the radiation from the sun to the earth through the intervening space devoid of matter. Similarly, the radiation from an open fire is another example of heat transfer. It is not generally recognized that radiation plays a very important role in the heat transfer at ordinary temperatures. Radiation is *not heat*. It is *changed* to heat when it strikes a solid object. It is estimated that about one-half of the heat transfer from a heated room to the inside surface of the outside walls takes place by direct radiation from interior objects and partition walls; the other half is the result of convection in the air near the exterior walls.

TYPE OF INSULATING MATERIAL

The various insulating materials commonly used in building construction may be divided into four general classes, according to their physical property, as:

1. Rigid.
2. Semi-rigid.
3. Flexible.
4. Fill.
5. Metal foil insulation.

Insulating products are manufactured from a great variety of raw materials. Those most commonly used are: *Asbestos, cork, cotton, gypsum, hair, jute, limestone, moss, paper pulp, wheat straw, wood,* and *aluminum.*

GENERAL CONSIDERATIONS

The primary reasons for application of insulating materials in homes are comfort and economy. When insulation is *properly* applied, it keeps the interior of the house at an even comfortable temperature which is obtained by a minimum of fuel consumption. Also, during the summer time, insulation helps to keep the rooms in all parts of the house comparatively cool and comfortable.

Similarly, if artificial cooling (air conditioning) is resorted to during the hot summer months, the plants may be operated with more economy if the building is properly insulated. Also, since insulation enhances the comfort and desirability of a building, it goes without saying that the well-insulated house has a higher loan and re-sale value than one not properly insulated.

Due to the various losses connected with the transfer of heat, only about 50 to 85% of the heat available in the fuel is actually transmitted to the part of the house where it is needed. The two predominant ways in which heat is lost is by leakage of cold air around and through doors, windows, and walls of the building, and by transmission through the material constituting the walls, floors and roof. It is evident that special precautions should be observed to reduce this leakage to a minimum.

When considering the economic factors involved in insulation, the full savings attained over a period of time usually will pay for its cost, as well as the expense connected with its installation. The factors that determine the length of this period are:

1. The cost of insulating material installed.
2. The value of the fuel saved.

In certain localities where the winters are long and severe (and where the fuel is expensive), the cost of insulation may pay for itself in a comparatively short time. In climates only moderately cold, or where the fuel is inexpensive, this time may be considerably longer.

RIGID-TYPE INSULATION

This type of insulation, often identified as *board insulation,* may be obtained in panels of various sizes. This type can be sawed and nailed in the same way as ordinary wood, as shown in Fig. 1. The rigid form is adapted to a wide range of uses in the construction of buildings, and it may be employed solely for its insulating value. Because of its rigidity, it is often utilized as a combination insulating and structural material, such as sheathing on the outside of framing members.

Rigid insulation is most commonly manufactured in panels 4-feet-wide and from 8- to 12-feet long, with a thickness of from one-half to one inch. Certain fibre and cork boards are produced in small panels ranging in width from one to two feet, with a length of from 2 1/2- to 5 1/2-feet. The thickness of these panels varies from one to three inches.

Application

When considering *frame construction* and *rigid insulation,* there are two general methods of installation:

1. Applied over the outside edge of framing members, such as wall studs, floor joists, and used with or without a covering of wood sheathing.
2. Applied between the framing members with an air space on each side.

Rigid Insulation Applied as Sheathing—When rigid insulation is used as wall sheathing under wood siding, shingles, brick veneer, or stucco, large panels are preferred. They may be cut to the size required and nailed directly to the framing members. The panels should be long enough to span the distance between sills and plates. Where this is impossible, the joints should be reinforced with a 2 $\times$ 4 to which the panel ends are nailed.

The edges and ends of the panels should be spaced approximately one-eighth or one-fourth of an inch apart, so that there will be no danger of buckling if swelling occurs. Bring the insulation in close contact with window and door frames. Fasten the panels to the framing, using nails specified by the insulation manufacturer. Beginning at the center of the panel, nail first to the intermediate studs, then around all edges, setting the nails approximately three-eighths of an inch from the edge. Space the nails from 4 to 6 inches apart. Drive them flush with the surface of the panel. The wall framework over which rigid insulation is applied as sheathing should be strengthened with corner bracing, the same as when horizontal wood sheathing is used. When using a brick or stone veneer, it is wise to use a tarred felt paper next to the insulating board, as shown in Fig. 2.

Rigid Insulation Applied Under Wood Sheathing—When utilizing this method of application, wood sheathing is applied directly over the insulating material and fastened to the framing members with nails one-half to 1-inch longer than ordinarily called for in uninsulated construction. In such cases, the nails in the insulating board may be spaced as much as 10 or 12 inches apart.

Insulation Used as a Plaster Base—Although directions for applying the different makes of materials when used as a plaster base vary according to the views of the manufacturers, the following suggestions are set forth as a general guide to the builder:

Plasterboard applied to framing members should be not more than 16 inches from center to center. Place the small size sheets with the length at right angles to the studs, joists, or rafters. End joints should center over the framing members. Bring the interlocking edges of adjacent sheets to moderate contact, but do not force into place. A space of approximately one-eighth to one-fourth inch should be left between the ends to prevent buckling. The end joints should be staggered.

A material called *vermiculite* has been developed which is a substitute for sand and is mixed with the plaster. This material is developed from a mica base which is exploded in size and, when mixed with plaster, forms a wall of small air pockets. These small air pockets formed in the plastered wall develops a rigid insulation base. The vermiculite material is very light in

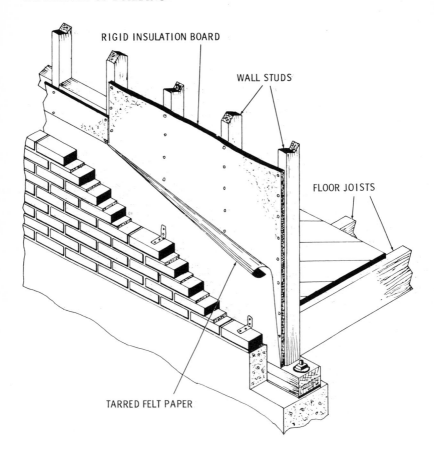

RIGID INSULATION BOARD

WALL STUDS

FLOOR JOISTS

TARRED FELT PAPER

Fig. 2. The installation of tarred felt paper over insulation board when using brick or stone veneer.

weight and therefore reduces the added weight in a conventional plastered wall or ceiling.

Rigid Insulation Used as Interior Finish—Panels of rigid insulating board for interior finish come in a variety of sizes. Any of the large sheets are 4-feet wide and in lengths up to 12 feet may be used. "Beveled tile" panels (all edges beveled), ranging in size from 12 × 12 to 16 × 48 inches, are also employed for this purpose. For best results, rigid insulating board for interior finish should be applied over framework, with the spacing not to exceed 16 inches between centers. Large panels, when applied with the length parallel to the studs, joists, or rafters, should be of sufficient length to span the height, length, or width of the room, as shown in Fig. 3.

There is grave danger of serious condensation in the cavities between the furring strips in installations of this kind. The inside surface should be effectively sealed with at least three coats of good oil paint. Adequate ventilation or mechanical dehumidification is used. All horizontal edges should be supported. The usual method of fastening large panels to the framing is as follows:

Beginning in the center, the boards are nailed to the intermediate studs, joists, or rafters with finishing nails approximately 1-1/2-inches long, spaced 4 to 6 inches. The nails are

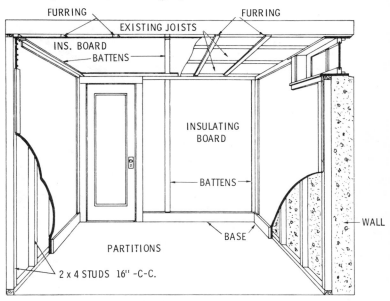

Fig. 3. Application of insulation board for interior finish in a typical basement room.

219

driven at a slight angle from the normal position, and counter-sunk. The edges of the panels are nailed with four-penny box nails, spaced 4 to 6 inches and set about 3/8 inch from the edge.

The panels should be spaced approximately 1/8 to 1/4 inch apart at all edges and ends. The joints must be battened. All building boards with wood or other organic bases shrink or swell with humidity changes, and large panels of soft insulating boards may tear themselves loose from the nails. Beveled-tile panels are applied with 1-inch finishing nails, spaced 4 to 6 inches on all edges and over intermediate supports, with heads countersunk into the material. The edges of adjacent pieces

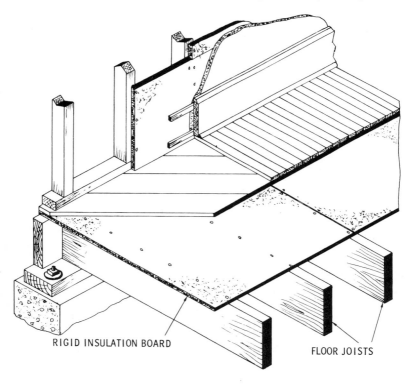

RIGID INSULATION BOARD

FLOOR JOISTS

Fig. 4. Application of rigid insulation board when applied under both finished floor and subfloor.

should be brought into moderate contact, but not forced into place. With this application, the joists need no further treatment, since the small panels with edges cut back present a pleasant and attractive appearance.

Rigid Insulation Used as an Insulation in Floors—In floors, rigid insulation generally is applied directly to the floor joists, with

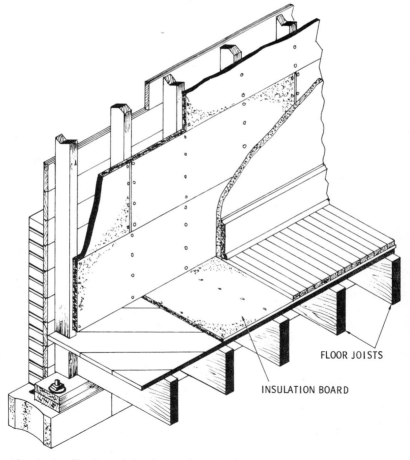

FLOOR JOISTS

INSULATION BOARD

Fig. 5. Application of insulation board when applied between finished floor and subfloor.

221

the sub-floor laid directly over the insulating material, as shown in Fig. 4. Large panels are preferred, although any size may be used. Since the insulation is not subjected to structural strain, it may be nailed only enough to hold it in place while the subfloor is being laid. A space of approximately 1/8 to 1/4 inch should be left at the joints for possible expansion. Rigid insulation may also be installed between the subfloor and the finish floor (Fig. 5). In this case, nailing is unnecessary since the sheets are held in place by the finish floor.

SEMIRIGID AND FELT-TYPE INSULATION

As the name suggests, this type of insulation is less rigid than the previously discussed rigid type, in that it possesses a certain amount of flexibility and serves primarily as a means of insulation. Most of the fibrous inorganic insulations, including the rock, slag, and glass wools, are available in felted semirigid forms, in thicknesses of 1 to 2 inches. Among the most valuable modern semirigid insulations are the foamed plastics—urethanes and styrenes. These boards have a very low density, less than 3 lbs. per cubic foot, very high compressive strength, greater than a ton per square foot, and enough rigidity that they can be handled in 2 × 8-ft. strips. Foamed-glass boards have slightly greater rigidity than the felted fiber boards, more resistance to compression, and slightly less insulating value. They are used for roof insulations under built-up covers, for insulation under slab-on-ground concrete floors, etc. As for the foamed plastics, they are rather brittle.

FLEXIBLE-TYPE INSULATION

This type of insulating material consists of a loosely felted, fibrous mat, usually covered on both sides with a layer of paper or fabric. It is sometimes referred to as *blanket* or *quilt* insulation. The paper covers are usually turned into thin flanges along the edges for nailing purposes. The outer cover may or may not be vapor-barring. When the vapor-barrier is desirable, the flanges are preferably lapped on the *edges* of the studs.

Flexible insulation is used solely for its insulating properties. Because of its nonstructural character, it will not serve as sheathing or as a plaster base; it is always used in addition to standard construction. Because of its light weight and loosely matted form, it is suitable for packing cracks around openings and for fitting into irregular shaped spaces. Flexible insulation is produced in strips approximately 15, 23, 31, and 35 inches wide, and in lengths up to 100 feet. The thickness ranges from 1 to 6 inches.

Application

The most common methods of installing flexible insulation in frame constructions, are:

1. Between framing members.
2. .Over the inside or outside edge of framing members.
3. Over the outside sheathing.

The insulation is often fastened to the framing or sheathing with ordinary lath nailing strips. In some cases, however, it may be convenient to utilize 1×2 lumber strips; in other cases, staples or large-headed nails are employed and nailing strips omitted. When flexible insulation is employed between framing members, a common method of installing it is to place it in the center of the air space between the studs of the wall, as shown in Fig. 6. This provides a dead-air space between the outside sheathing and the insulation, and between the inside finish and the insulation.

FILL-TYPE INSULATION

This type of insulation is powdered, granulated, or shredded material. It comes in bulk lots and, as the name implies, is used for filling spaces in wall, floor, and ceiling construction. Fill material can be applied in houses under construction, or those already completed, by packing or blowing it into the spaces between the framing members. Its insulating value varies with the properties of the raw materials used, and according to the density with which the material is packed. Fill insulation is usually placed between studs, ceiling joists, and roof rafters, where it fills spaces of considerable size.

METAL-FOIL INSULATION

Metal foil is a form of insulating material which consists of a sheet of metal, usually aluminum, which is either applied in its

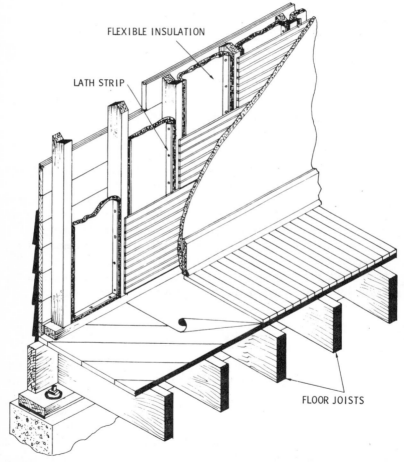

FLEXIBLE INSULATION

LATH STRIP

FLOOR JOISTS

Fig. 6. Example of installation of flexible insulation between wall studs.

original form as a thin foil or in combination with a backing of composition board or paper. In sheet form, the foil is applied by crinkling the sheets and applying two or more between the studding of walls or between the joists under the floors.

The theory involved in all uses of aluminum for insulation is the unusual property of reflection of radiation. Highly polished metals are the most efficient materials for purpose of radiation. Since it is a well known fact that all metals have a very high thermal conductivity, and since reflection is exclusively a superficial function, the thickness of the metals used for insulation may be reduced to the practical minimum. The reason for the utilization of aluminum for this purpose is because highly polished aluminum has a highly reflective surface and, unlike most other

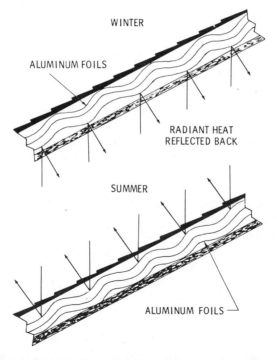

Fig. 7. Diagram showing how aluminum foil, when installed as shown, will reflect radiation from the inside during winter, and reflect solar radiation during winter and summer.

225

bright materials, retains its reflectivity practically undiminished under most atmospheric conditions.

Aluminum foil may be applied to structural material or insulation, or it may be used to divide an air space. When used to divide an air space, several sheets of foil may be separated by a skeleton framework of wood or other material, or by sheets of corrugated paper. When the air space is to be divided only once or twice, aluminum foil on heavy paper may be nailed between the studs, joists, or rafters.

Foil must *never* be applied on or near the cold sides of walls. It is highly conductive, and almost a perfect vapor-barrier. It attains temperatures below the dew-point of the humid air inside the house, and serious condensation troubles are often set up. The same thing is true of vapor-barring polyvinyl films. *Keep all vapor-barriers away from the cold sides of walls.*

INSULATING A FINISHED BUILDING

As a rule, it may be said that while the insulation can not be applied with the same economy and convenience as when the house is being built, certain parts of nearly every house can be insulated with a considerable advantage in comfort. Because every case may differ, depending upon the condition of the house and the use to which it is subjected, it is not possible to follow any general plan in insulation of this kind.

Assuming for example, however, that an attic room needs to be insulated, an examination of the construction of the house will reveal if the floor or roof areas are accessible. If the space between the ceiling and roof is so small that it makes it difficult to apply insulation over the entire area, it may be found feasible to apply fill insulation, which can be blown or poured between the rafters and attic floor joists, and in this manner it will be most practicable. If, on the other hand, the entire floor or roof area is readily accessible, any type of insulation may be used in the same manner as that of new construction.

When considering the side walls of the existing house, various problems will be encountered, and it is usually found that the fill-in method is most suitable for wood frame construction. Among other methods used are:

1. Application of rigid insulation to the inside surfaces as an interior finish or as a base for plaster, paint, or wall paper.
2. Application of either rigid or flexible material to the outside of the house with a new exterior finish placed over the insulating material.

Of these two methods, the use of rigid insulation boards on the outside wall surfaces possibly will be found to be the most economical. Thin insulations of any type have limited usefulness, and they may not be worth making extensive and expensive major alterations.

It will be necessary in most cases, however, to remove the inside trim around windows and doors, and when replacing it, to insert woodfiller strips which will take care of the added thickness of the walls. The job may or may not be worth the trouble.

REDUCING LEAKAGE AROUND DOORS AND WINDOWS

A large amount of the heat delivered to the rooms is lost by air leakage around doors and windows. Another large factor in heat loss is the heat leakage through the window glass.

These various heat losses may be greatly prevented by:

1. Caulking.
2. Weather strips.
3. Storm or double-glass windows.

Though the house may have been tight when built, a few years of usage will sometimes permit a considerable amount of leakage. In addition, small cracks often develop in masonry walls which, in time, may become sufficiently large to permit a considerable air leakage.

Caulking

The most common remedy against this air leakage is found in caulking or filling of the leaks. The most satisfactory results are obtained when the "staff-bead," if any, is removed from the outside of the frame and oakum or jute packed solidly into the cracks around the frame. Then caulking compound is placed next to the oakum or jute in the remaining space and the staff-bead replaced, in this manner tightly sealing the crack. In cases where it is impractical to remove the staff-bead, the space between this strip and the masonry wall is filled with caulking compound.

Weather Strips

In the same manner as caulking reduces air leakage around window and door frames, so does weather strips minimize leakage due to loose fittings. Permanent efficient weather strips consist of narrow pieces of metal especially designed for use around door and window frames. Strips of felt tightly packed around the outside of a window frame, sash, or door will give at least temporary relief.

Double-Glass Windows

In locations where the weather is severe, a common method to prevent heat leakage through the window glass is to double the glass, either by installing storm windows or by insertion of an additional pane in the original frame. This is the only present known method in eliminating heat transfer through the glass of windows, skylights, etc. In some cases, triple glazing with dead air spaces between the panes has been found to be a more satisfactory method of insulation. It is *not,* however, *twice* as effective as double-glazing. Double-glazing in the same sash is rarely satisfactory. The accepted method is to use the commercial double or triple panes with thin-air-spaces between and the edges fused or sealed.

WHERE TO INSULATE

To reduce heat loss from the house during cold weather, all walls, ceilings, roofs, and floors that separate heated from unheated spaces should be insulated. Insulation should be placed on all outside walls and in the ceiling as shown in Fig. 8. In houses involving unheated crawl spaces, insulation should be placed between the floor joists. If a bulk type of insulation is used, it should be well supported by slats with galvanized mesh wire or by a rigid board. Reflective insulation is often used for insulation of crawl spaces. Crawl spaces, as well as attic spaces, should be

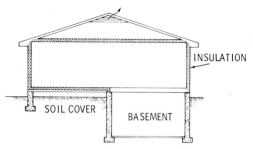

Fig. 8. *Illustrating the proper way to insulate walls, floors, and ceilings.*

well ventilated. A ground cover of roll roofing may also be placed on the soil of crawl spaces to decrease the moisture content of the space.

In 1-1/2-story houses, insulation should be placed along all areas that are adjacent to unheated areas, as shown in Fig. 9. These include stairways, dwarf walls, and dormers. Provisions should be made for ventilation of the unheated areas. Where attic

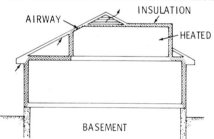

Fig. 9. *A method of insulating 1 1/2-story houses.*

storage space is unheated and a stairway is included, insulation should be used around the stairway as well as in the first floor ceiling, as shown in Fig. 10. The door leading to the attic should be weather stripped to prevent the loss of heat. Walls adjoining an unheated garage or porch should be well insulated.

In houses with flat or low-pitched roofs, as shown in Fig. 11, insulation should be used in the ceiling area with sufficient space allowed above for a clear ventilating area between the joists. Insulation should be used along the perimeter of a house built on a slab. A vapor barrier should be included under the slab. Insulation can be used effectively to improve comfort conditions within

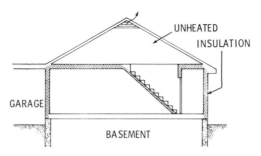

Fig. 10. Illustrating a method of shielding a heated area from an unheated area by insulating.

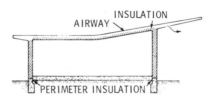

Fig. 11. Insulation of a typical flat roof house.

the house during hot weather. These surfaces exposed to the direct rays of the sun may attain temperatures of 50°F or more above shade temperature and, of course, tend to transfer this heat towards the inside of the house. Insulation in the roofs and walls retards the flow of heat and, consequently, less heat is transmitted through such surfaces.

Where any system of cooling hot-weather air is used, insulation should be used in all exposed ceilings and walls in the same manner as for preventing heat loss in cold weather. Of course, where cooling is used, the windows and doors should be kept closed during periods when outdoor temperatures are above inside temperatures. Windows exposed to the sun should be shaded with awnings.

Ventilation of attic and roof space is an important adjunct to insulation. Without ventilation, an attic space may become very hot and hold the heat for many hours. Obviously, more heat will be transmitted through the ceiling when the attic temperature is 150°F than if it is 120°F. Ventilation methods suggested for protection against cold-weather condensation apply equally well to protection against excessive hot-weather roof temperature.

INSTALLATION OF INSULATION

Blanket insulation should be placed between framing members so that the tabs lap all edges, including both bottom and top plates, as shown in Fig. 12. Where the vapor barrier on the insulation does not cover the framing member, a vapor barrier paper should be used over these unprotected areas. A hand stapling machine is usually used to fasten insulation tabs and vapor barriers in place. Batt insulation is also placed between framing members (studs or joists) and is fastened with staples. Because of the shorter lengths of the batts, they should be placed so that the

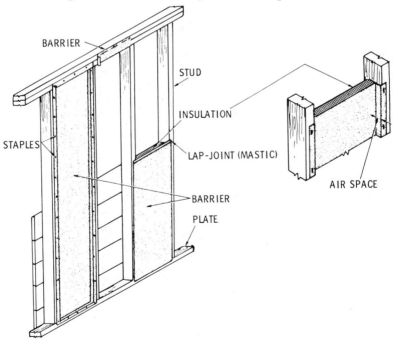

BARRIER

STUD

INSULATION

STAPLES

LAP-JOINT (MASTIC)

BARRIER

PLATE

AIR SPACE

Fig. 12. Illustrating blanket insulation placed between joists or studs.

231

barriers lap each other and the lap should be sealed. When batts do not include a vapor barrier, the barrier should be stapled to framing members from bottom to top plate.

Reflective insulation, when used in a single-sheet form, should be placed so as to divide the space formed by the framing members into two approximately equal spaces. Some reflective insulations include air spaces and are furnished with nailing tabs. This type is fastened in place much like blanket insulation. Fill insulation is poured or blown into place (Fig. 13). A vapor

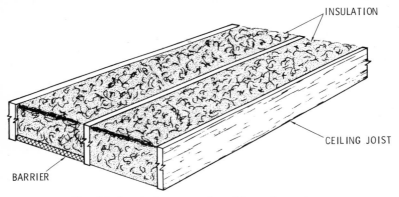

Fig. 13. Insulation poured or blown into place.

barrier should be used on the warm side (the bottom, in case of ceiling joists) before insulation is placed.

PRECAUTIONS IN INSULATING

There are areas around window and door openings, shown in Fig. 14, that also require insulation. Insulation should be used between the window jamb and the rough opening as well as under the sill. To complete the job, a vapor barrier should be stapled in place to cover all surfaces not covered by the barrier of the blanket insulation.

In two-story houses, the area at joist ends should also be insulated and have a vapor barrier (Fig. 15). This precaution also applies to first-floor joists in the area above the foundation walls. The insulation should be fitted around the electrical outlet boxes, and the vapor barrier must be tight against their outer edges to prevent the escape of water vapor.

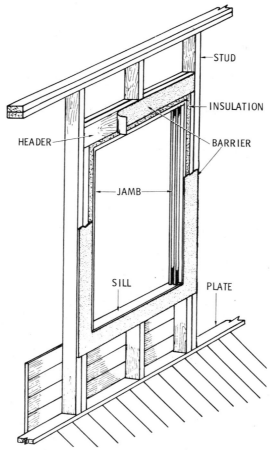

Fig. 14. Insulation around wall openings.

VAPOR BARRIERS

Most building materials are permeable to water vapor. In cold climates during cold weather such vapor, generated in the house from cooking, dishwashing, laundering, bathing, humidifiers, and

233

other sources, may pass through wall and ceiling materials and condense in the wall or attic space, where it may subsequently

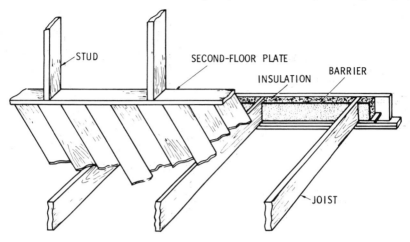

Fig. 15. Insulating joist space in outside walls.

do damage to exterior paint and interior finish, or may even cause decay in structural members. As a protection, a material highly resistive to vapor transmission, called a *vapor barrier,* should be used on the warm side of a wall or below the insulation in a roof. Among the effective vapor barrier materials are such products as paper coated on both sides with asphalt and sold in rolls of 500 square feet weighing about 50 pounds per roll, single- or double-faced aluminum-foil type of reflective insulation, aluminum-foil backed gypsum lath, and fiberboard lath coated on the back with asphalt.

Asphalt-laminated paper makes a good barrier for use back of dry-wall finishes, but should not be used where the paper could become wet during construction. Prolonged wetting damages such paper, and its value as a barrier may be lost. Wetting of paper may occur back of metal lath or back of plaster where the plaster is applied during cold weather.

Some types of blanket insulation have a barrier material on one side of the blanket. Such blankets should be attached with the tabs at their sides fastened on the faces of the studs, and the blanket should be cut long enough so that the cover sheet can lap over the face of the soleplate at the bottom and over the plate at the top of the stud space. Where the membrane type of vapor barrier is used, it should be applied vertically over the face of the studs and tacked down. The lath or wall finish is then applied over the vapor barrier. Vapor barriers should be cut to fit tightly around electric outlets and switch boxes. Any cold-air returns to the furnace in outside walls should be lined with tin.

Paint coatings on plaster may be very effective as vapor barriers if materials are properly chosen and applied. They don't, however, offer protection during the period of construction, and moisture may cause paint blisters on exterior paint before the interior paint can be applied. This is most likely to happen in buildings that are constructed during periods when outdoor temperatures are 25°F. or more below inside temperatures. Paint coatings cannot be considered a substitute for the membrane types of vapor barriers, but they do provide a good degree of protection for houses where other types of vapor barriers were not installed during construction.

Of the various types of paint, one coat of aluminum primer followed by two decorative coats of flat wall or lead and oil paint is quite effective. For rough plaster or for buildings in very cold climates, two coats of the aluminum primer may be necessary. A primer and sealer of the pigmented type followed by decorative finish coats or two coats of rubber-base paint are also effective in retarding vapor transmission. For dry-wall construction where plywood, fiberboard, or other wall materials are used in place of plaster, paint coatings may be applied to the back or to the face. Asphalt coatings on the back of plywood, for example, make an excellent barrier. Two coats, or enough to make a bright, shiny surface, are required.

Since no type of vapor barrier can be considered 100 percent resistive, and since some vapor leakage into the wall may be expected, it is important that the flow of vapor to the outside should not be impeded by materials of relatively high vapor resistance on the cold side of the vapor barrier. For example, sheathing paper should be of a type that is waterproof but not highly vapor resistant. Tarred felt meets this requirement.

VENTILATION

Condensation of moisture vapor may occur in attic spaces and under flat roofs during cold weather. Even where vapor barriers are used, it is to be expected that some vapor will work into these spaces around pipes and other inadequately protected areas and some through the vapor barrier itself. Although the amount might be unimportant if equally distributed, it is likely to be concentrated in some cold spot in sufficient quantity to cause damage. Most types of roofings are highly resistant to vapor movement, and little vapor can escape through the roofing itself. The most practical method of removing the moisture is by adequately ventilating the roof spaces.

During cold weather, a warm attic combined with exposure to sun may provide enough heat to cause snow on the roof to melt, but without the extra heat from the attic the snow at the eaves does not melt. Water from the roof will then form ice dams at the gutter and roof overhang and may cause water to back up at the eaves into the walls and ceilings. Similar dams often form in roof valleys. With a well-insulated ceiling and adequate ventilation, attic temperatures are low and melting over the attic space will be reduced.

In hot weather, ventilation of attic and roof spaces offers an effective means of removing hot air and thereby lowering the temperature in these spaces. Insulation should be used in the ceilings below the attic or roof space to further retard heat flow into the rooms below and materially improve comfort conditions.

It is a common practice to install louvered openings in the end walls of gable roofs for ventilation. Air movement through such openings is dependent primarily on wind direction and velocity, and no appreciable movement can be expected when there is no wind or unless one or more openings face toward the wind. More positive air movement can be obtained by providing openings at the eave line in addition to openings near the ridge. The differences in temperature between the attic and the outside will then create an air movement independent of the wind and also a more positive movement when there is wind. Where there is a crawl space under the house or porch, ventilation is necessary to remove moisture vapor rising from the soil. Such moisture vapor may otherwise condense on the wood below the floor and facilitate decay.

SUMMARY

Insulation is a material used to prevent the high outside temperature from entering the house during the summer time, and prevents the inside higher temperature from leaving the building during the winter time. Insulation of a building is usually concerned with the problem of reducing the transfer of heat from one region to another, and is generally called thermal insulation.

The primary reasons for application of insulating materials in homes are comfort and economy. When insulation is properly applied, it keeps the interior of the house at an even comfortable temperature with a minimum of fuel consumption. Also, in the summer months, insulation helps to keep the rooms in all parts of the house comparatively cool and comfortable. If air conditioning is used during the hot season, the system may be operated with more economy if the building is properly insulated.

There are various types of insulating materials used. One of the most common materials used for insulation in homes is the rigid-type insulation board. Rigid insulation is most commonly manufactured in panels 4-feet wide and from 8-to-12-feet long, with a thickness of from one-half to one inch. Because of its rigidity, it is often used as a combination insulating and structural material, such as sheathing on the outside of framing members.

Fill-type insulation materials are powdered, granulated, or shredded, and come in bulk lots. This type of insulation can be applied in houses under construction, or in those already completed, by packing or blowing it into the space between the framing members. Fill insulation is generally placed between studs, ceiling joists, and roof rafters.

The best insulation and its application will be of little help if air leakage around doors and windows is not controlled. The most common remedy against this air leakage is found in caulking or

filling of the leaks. Many types of caulking compounds are manufactured for various building materials, and the best compound
for general use is the type which never hardens, chips, or cracks.

REVIEW QUESTIONS

1. By what three methods is heat transferred?
2. Name the various insulating materials.
3. How is fill insulation applied in a house?
4. What is a vapor barrier?
5. What is the purpose of insulation?

CHAPTER 15

Scaffolding and Staging

A *scaffold* is a platform built against the side of a building or steeple for the support of workmen. *Staging* is an elevated platform built against the side of a building for the same purpose. A scaffold is a one-story structure serving to support workmen on a low building, whereas staging is a more substantial structure progressively built up as the erection of tall buildings proceed, the name staging being applied because it is built up in "stages", or one story at a time.

These structures are temporary, to provide an elevated support or floor, where work can be carried on. Many accidents occur annually through faulty or incomplete scaffolding. The design and construction of these structures should be done by experienced men, and no attempt should be made to economize by the use of inferior lumber and by inadequate nailing. Where extensive scaffolding is necessary, it is frequently economical to use sectional pipe scaffolding, which may be obtained from supply firms on a rental basis. Many contractors, especially masonry and plastering contractors, possess their own. For interior use, such as by painters, decorators, and installers of electric fixtures, the scaffolding may have large casters to permit moving without dismantling. In scaffolding large auditoriums and churches for decorating, a full carload of lumber is often required if nailed scaffolding is to be used. It is important that the lumber should be selected for straight grain and freedom from shakes or knots.

SCAFFOLDING

There is a great variety of scaffolds to meet the varied conditions encountered in building. In general, with respect to the method of support, they may be classed as:

1. Supported.
2. Cantilever.
3. Bracket.
4. Suspended or hanging.

Recently the Department of Labor (Bureau of Labor Standards) established some minimum requirements for safety and health regulations for construction. To meet the requirement set forth by the agency, scaffolding should:

1. Have guard rails and toeboard on the open side and ends of scaffolds.
2. Scaffold planks should extend over the end supports by 6 inches.
3. The scaffold poles should bear on an adequate foundation.
4. Diagonal braces should be placed in both directions across the face of the scaffolds.
5. The platform planks should be laid close together.

Supported Scaffolds

A simple form of supported scaffold is shown in Fig. 1, as used in the erection of wooden buildings. The scaffold illustrated consists of uprights, outriggers, cleats, and planks forming a platform. The various parts are fastened together, as shown. Where there are more than two platform levels requiring more substantial construction, and each upright consisting of more than one length, the structure becomes a *staging*, as distinguished from a scaffold.

Framed Portable Supported Scaffolds

Frequently, as in the repair or decoration of ceilings in churches and other public buildings, a self-contained portable scaffold which may be easily moved is required. A form of such construction, consisting of four uprights, cross and diagonal braces, is shown in Fig. 2. This frame structure may be adapted to outside work by somewhat heavier construction.

Cantilever Scaffolds

In this type of scaffold, the platform is supported by beams which project through openings in the wall frame (resting on window sills or other horizontal members), with the inner ends secured as shown in Fig. 3. These ends may be secured by hook irons, as at *A*, passing around one joist, or by a vertical wooden

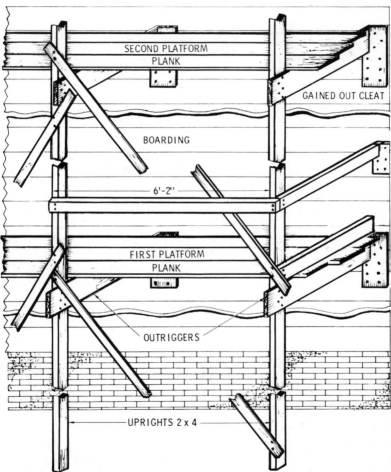

Fig. 1. Simple scaffold built on the side of a wooden building consisting of uprights.

241

piece *D* attached to the beam and to a saddle B, engaging with two joists as shown.

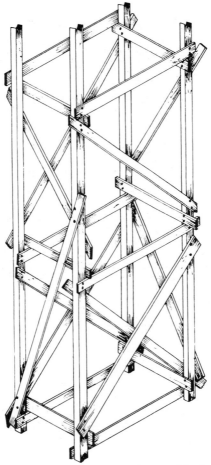

Fig. 2. Detail of framed portable scaffold suitable for interior work.

Bracket Scaffolds

This is an inexpensive and convenient form of scaffold which requires little lumber and is semiportable. It can be moved from one position to another by removing the bolts which fasten it to the wall frame. As shown in Fig. 4, the bracket has two studs

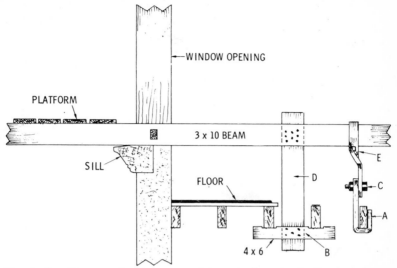

Fig. 3. Cantilever scaffold supported by openings in the wall and anchored down by interior building construction.

running between the horizontal and vertical members, with two hook bolts arranged to pass around a stud and through the sheathing. Another form of bracket scaffold, designed to be supported on window sills, or horizontal members of the wall frame, is shown in Fig. 5.

Suspended or Hanging Scaffolds

This form of scaffold is generally employed by painters and in erecting for cornice work. The simplest is the ladder scaffold, consisting of planks laid on the rungs of a ladder forming a platform suspended by two double iron hooks fastened to block-and-fall rigging, as shown in Fig. 6.

STAGING

In tall buildings, it is evident that some type of construction heavier and stronger than ordinary scaffolding must be employed. A construction permitting vertical additions as the building rises story by story is necessary. Such a construction is known as *staging,* as distinguished from a scaffold, presumably because it is

243

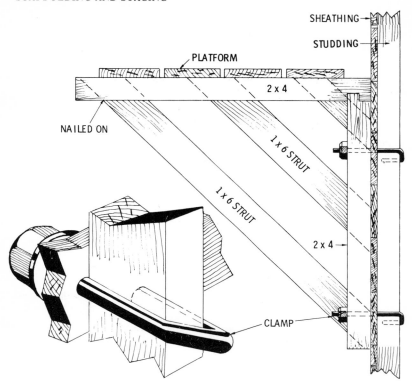

Fig. 4. Bracket scaffold supported by construction walls.

erected in successive stages as the construction of the building progresses.

A typical staging is shown in Fig. 7. Aside from its use in the construction of tall buildings, staging is also largely employed in bridge and viaduct construction. In such cases, the staging is generally about the height of the springing of the arch and is used to support the center, or as a platform to connect the different sections of girders, etc.

SUMMARY

Scaffolding is a platform built against the side of a building for the use of workmen. Staging is an elevated platform built against the side of a building for the same purpose. Scaffolding is a one-

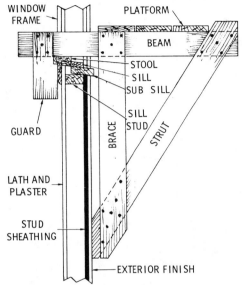

Fig. 5. Bracket scaffold supported by window sills.

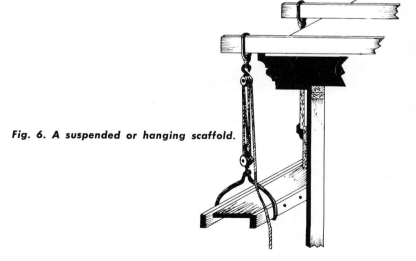

Fig. 6. A suspended or hanging scaffold.

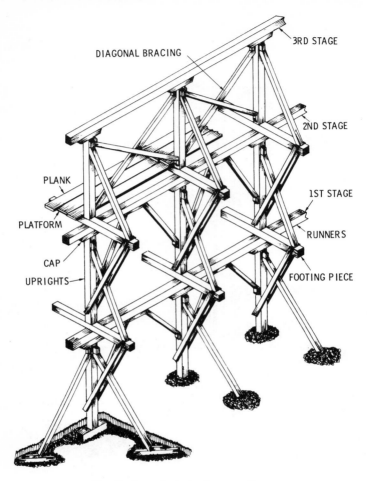

DIAGONAL BRACING

3RD STAGE

2ND STAGE

PLANK

1ST STAGE

PLATFORM

RUNNERS

CAP

UPRIGHTS

FOOTING PIECE

Fig. 7. A typical staging erection.

story structure serving to support workmen, while staging is a more substantial structure progressively built up as the erection of the building progresses.

Many accidents occur annually through faulty or incomplete scaffolding. The construction of these structures should never be made with inferior material just to economize. Many contractors purchase or rent sectional pipe scaffolding which is installed and removed quickly and is generally safe for workmen.

Aside from staging used in the construction of tall buildings, it is also largely employed in bridge and viaduct construction. In many cases the staging is used to support the center or as a platform to connect the different sections of girders.

REVIEW QUESTIONS

1. What is the difference between scaffolding and staging?
2. What are the four methods of support for scaffolding?
3. What are the dangers in inadequate scaffolding?
4. Why is pipe scaffolding safer?

CHAPTER 16

Hoisting Apparatus

The term *hoist* is defined as a machine for raising or lowering heavy or bulky articles. In the construction of buildings, some form of hoist is almost always necessary, as for instance in placing heavy girders, sections of wall frames, roof trusses, etc. In any hoist, means must be provided for attaching the load. Proper reduction gearing must be obtained between the load and point at which the power is applied, depending upon the intensity of the applied force. The various forms of hoist used by builders may be classified:

1. With respect to the lifting medium, as:
   (a.) Rope.
   (b.) Chain.
2. With respect to the form of gearing, as:
   (a.) Pulley (block-and-fall).
   (b.) Differential.
   (c.) Spur gear and drum.
   (d.) Spur gear and spool.
3. With respect to the supporting structure, as:
   (a.) Gin pole.
   (b.) Tripod or shear legs.
   (c.) Stiff-leg mast.
   (d.) Derrick, etc.
4. With respect to the drive, as:
   (a.) Hand.
   (b.) Steam.
   (c.) Electric, etc.

ROPES

Manila, cotton, or wire is used in the manufacture of ropes. Manila is stronger and more durable than cotton, and is used for light-duty hoisting, as with block and tackle. Wire rope is used for heavy-duty hoisting. When the rope is to be handled a great deal,

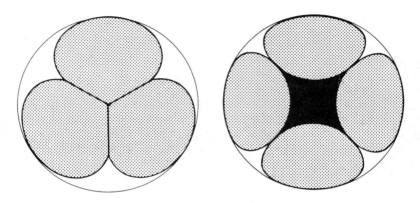

Fig. 1. End view of three- and four-strand rope.

cotton rope is easy on the hands. Rope is manufactured in three, four, or more strands, as shown in Fig. 1. In the three-strand rope, the strands are larger than in the four-strand rope. The four-strand is stronger and more pliable, and has an even surface. The four-strand rope weighs more per foot, and is constructed on a center core, which keeps the strands away from the center, thus reducing chafing as the rope is bent around a pulley.

The extra cost of the four-strand rope is justified if the rope is properly cared for. When a weight is hung upon the end of a rope, the tendency is for the rope to untwist and become longer. In making a rope, it is impossible to make these strains exactly balance each other. It is this fact that makes it necessary to take out the *turns* in a new rope. The amount of twist that should be put in the yarns has been ascertained approximately by experience.

In Table 1, the figures refer to average grade manila rope, new and without knots. It should be noted that *knots* weaken a rope. The safe load given in the table is the greatest load that a single rope should carry, being about 1/7 of the breaking load. Wire rope (if made flexible) with a hemp core to each strand, and a central hemp core to the rope itself, will stand a strain in pounds approximately equal to the square of the circumference in inches multiplied by 600. Thus, a wire rope termed "three-quarters,"

Table 1. Properties of Three Strand Manila Rope

I	II	III	IV		V	VI	VII
Diameter (Inches)	Circumference (Inches)	Weight of 100 feet of rope (Pounds)	Length of each pound of rope Ft.	Ins.	Safe load (Pounds)	Breaking load (Pounds)	Diameter of pulley (Inches)
3/16	9/16	2	50	0	35	230	1½
¼	¾	3	33	4	55	400	2
5/16	1	4	25	0	90	630	2½
⅜	1⅛	5	20	0	130	900	3
7/16	1¼	6	16	8	175	1,240	3½
½	1½	7⅔	13	0	230	1,620	4
⅝	2	13⅓	7	6	410	2,880	5
¾	2¼	16⅓	6	1	520	3,640	6
⅞	2¾	23⅔	4	3	775	5,440	7
1	3	28⅓	3	6	925	6,480	8
1⅛	3½	38	2	7	1,260	8,820	9
1¼	3¾	45	2	2	1,445	10,120	10
1⅜	4¼	58	1	8	1,855	13,000	11
1½	4½	65	1	6	2,085	14,600	12
1¾	5¼	97	1	0	3,070	21,500	14
2	6	113	0	10	3,600	25,200	16
2½	7½	184	0	6½	5,630	39,400	20
3	9	262	0	4½	8,100	56,700	24

with a diameter of about 3/4 inch and a circumference of 2 1/4 inches, will safely stand 3037.5 lbs., having a factor of safety of seven. Wire ropes should be kept free of rust, and should be lubricated with graphite when running. The rope should be oiled occasionally with raw linseed oil, well rubbed in.

So-called flexible wire ropes should not be worked around a sheave or drum having a diameter less than six times the girth of the rope. Stronger ropes, which are used for winding from great depths, should not pass over any wheel of a less diameter than ten times the circumference. The smaller figures are for ropes worked at a slow speed only. For each increase in speed, the pulley should also be enlarged. This must especially be insisted upon with elevators and lifts, in which case it is advisable to use ten as a minimum ratio.

Ropes and cordage are so peculiarly a sailor's province that nautical expressions must necessarily be used. Accordingly, a few explanations will be given of terms used in this connection:

Belay—To make fast the end of a tackle, fall, etc., at the conclusion of a hoisting operation or the like.

Bend—A fastening of one rope to another or to a ring, thimble, etc.

Bight—The loose part of a rope between two fixed ends.

Haul—To heave or pull on a rope.

Hitch—A fastening of a rope simply by winding it, without knotting, around some object.

Knot—A fastening of one part of a rope to another part of the same, by interlacing them and drawing the loops tight.

Lay—To twist strands together, as in rope making, the fibre or tow receiving a right-handed twist to make yarns, yarns being laid

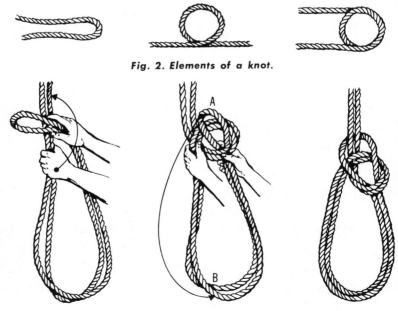

Fig. 2. Elements of a knot.

Fig. 3. Bowline knot made in the middle of the rope.

left handed into strands, and strands right handed into ropes. Three strands make a hawser, and three hawsers are laid up into a cable.

Make fast—To secure the loose end of a rope to some fixed object.

Marline spike—A long tapered steel instrument used to unlay or separate the strands of rope for splicing, etc., or for working marline around a seizing.

Parcelled—Wrapped with canvas, rags, leather, etc., to resist chafing.

Seize—To lash a rope permanently with a smaller cord.

Serve—To lash with cord, etc., wound tightly and continuously around the object.

Splice—To connect rope ends together by unlaying the strands of each then plaiting both together so as to make one continuous whole.

Strand—Two or more large yarns twisted together.

Taut—Stretched or drawn tight, strained.

Yarn—Fibres twisted together.

THEORY OF KNOTS

The principle of a knot is "no two parts which would move in the same direction, if the rope were to slip, should lie along side of and touch each other." Another principle that should be added to the above is that a knot or a hitch must be so devised

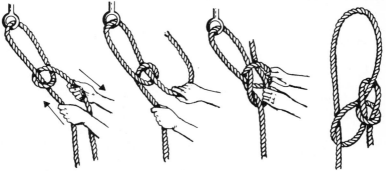

Fig. 4. Bowline knot made at the end of the rope.

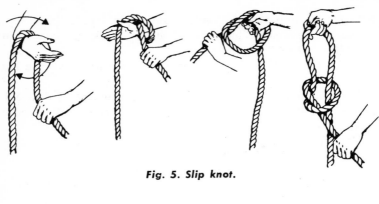

Fig. 5. Slip knot.

Fig. 6. Figure-eight knot.   Fig. 7. Stevedore knot.

that the *tight part of the rope must bear on the free end in such a manner as to pinch and hold it against another tight part of the rope, or in a hitch, against the object to which the rope is attached.*

The elements of a knot or bends that a rope undergoes in the formation of a knot or of a hitch are of three kinds.

1. Bight.
2. Loop or turn.
3. Round turn.

These are shown in Fig. 2. Knots and hitches are made by combining these elements in different ways, conforming to the principles of a knot given previously. Figs. 3 through 17 show different kinds of knots used in hoisting apparatus.

Fig. 8. Timber-hitch knot.

Fig. 9. Half-hitch knot.

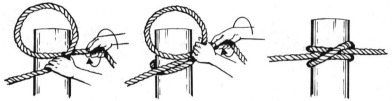

Fig. 10. Clove hitch, sailors method.

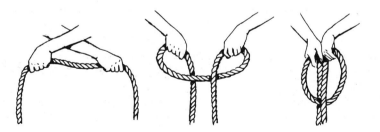

Fig. 11. Clove hitch, circus method.

EFFECT OF KNOTS

A rope is weakened by knots. In order to form a knot, the rope must be bent, which brings most of the strain on the outside fibers. The overloading breaks the outside fibers, increasing the

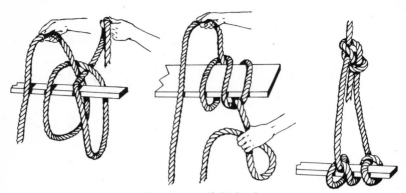

Fig. 12. Scaffold hitch.

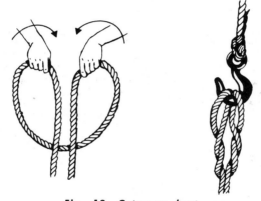

Fig. 13. Cats-paw knot.

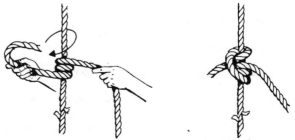

Fig. 14. Taut line or rolling hitch, which can be used to support a taut rope with broken strands.

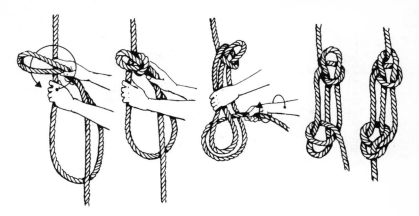

Fig. 15. Sheepshank knot.

Fig. 16. Anchor bend.

strain on the fibers below, which later break and soon the entire rope breaks. From experiments, the approximate efficiency of knots, hitches, and splices varies as follows: straight rope, 100%; eye splice over an iron eye, 90%; short splice, 80%; timber hitch anchor bend, 65%; clove hitch running bowline, 60%; overhand knot, 45%.

TREATMENT OF ROPE ENDS

The process of building up a rope from strands is called *laying* a rope, and so twisting together strands that have become untwisted is called *relaying*. *Whipping* consists in binding the end of a rope with twine to prevent it untwisting, as in Fig. 18. Ropes that are to be passed through pulley blocks or through small holes

257

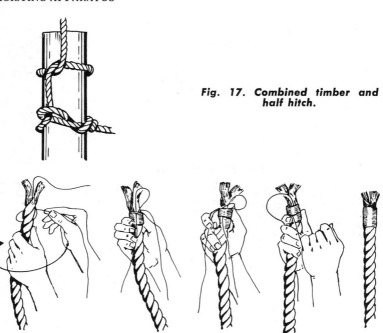

Fig. 17. Combined timber and half hitch.

Fig. 18. Whipping the end of a rope.

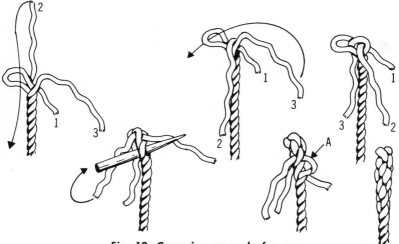

Fig. 19. Crowning an end of a rope.

should be finished in this way. A method of doing this so that both ends of the twine are fastened is shown in Fig. 18.

CROWNING

This is a neat, secure, and permanent method of fastening the strands of a rope when a slight enlargement of the end is not an objection. Fig. 19 shows how this is done.

EMERGENCY TRIP SLING

It is sometimes desirable to use a sling that can be tripped and the load dropped without slacking up on the hoisting rope, as is done with a regular trip sling for hay. If such a sling is not at hand, a substitute may be made as follows:

Procure a piece of rope of sufficient length, splice or tie the ends together to make it endless, draw the loop out long, and lay on it the material to be raised. Pull the sling up around the load and lay one end of the sling on the double ropes of the other end, as is done in Fig. 3.

CARE OF ROPES

Hemp is easily rotted by dampness; hence, if the ropes have been used in the rain or allowed to get into water, they must be hung up to dry. A beam eight or ten feet above ground within a shed is most convenient for this purpose. The rope is passed over the beam from one side to another, and is permitted to hang down in loose festoons on each side, well clear of the ground. This facilitates the circulation of the air around each part of the rope. Under no circumstances should a rope be coiled when wet, as the internal covered parts absorb all the moisture and will quickly rot.

Constant inspection is necessary, and a good method of inspecting the inside fibers is by partially untwisting the strands. This gives an opportunity of examining the inside of the strands. Strain and chafing will cause the fibers to rupture. Much of· this trouble may be prevented in the case of standing ropes by using parcelling or chafing gear, made of marline or leather fastened around the rope to protect it. Always suspect a rope that has lain in a warm place, such as a boiler house. It may have "perished" and is not trustworthy. Ropes that have to be exposed to water are rendered more durable by coating the yarn with tar. This, however, reduces the strength of the rope by one-fourth.

It may be advisable to state here that rope makers generally specify all their ropes in terms of the circumference, and the various formula for weight and strength are all calculated from that dimension.

ROPE WEIGHTS

Manila, or wire rope for hoisting is usually provided with a rope weight or *cow-sucker*, as shown in Fig. 20. The object of this weight is to cause the rope to pay out when released.

CHAINS

Chains are made of round bar iron or steel forged into links by bending to shape and welding. The stud is a distance piece, usually of cast steel, which serves to strengthen the link; it is used on the larger sizes alone and permits a longer link. Most chains for heavy stresses are made this way. A length of stud chain is illustrated in Fig. 21, and is noteworthy because of the swivel in the middle of its length, permitting rotary motion without fouling the chain. A chain or cable shackle, as seen in Fig. 22, is used for connecting lengths (usually 15 fathoms) of a cable. The bolt has a countersunk head and is locked by a wooden or brass taper pin.

GEARING

Combination of Pulleys

The mere passing of a rope over one fixed pulley for hoisting a weight does not give any increase of power. The combination of ropes and pulleys used to gain a mechanical advantage in lifting a load is known as a block and tackle. The block consists of a shell, pulleys, and a hook or an eye. Usually, two blocks are used. A rope or chain is used for connecting the blocks.

The block and tackle gives a mechanical advantage in the application of power. It is easier to haul downward on a pull of 100 lbs. than it is to lift 100 lbs. directly from the ground. This advantage should not be confused with mechanical advantage or multiplication of effort. According to the degree of gearing, the 100-lb. weight may be lifted by the application of less force as 50, 25, 10, 5 lbs. of pull, etc. For instance, when one end of the rope is fixed and passes under a single pulley to which the load is attached, and the free end is lifted, the travel of the rope or cord

Fig. 20. Rope weight or cow-sucker.

is double that of the weight. The power necessary to sustain the latter is half the weight, less friction. It may be stated in the reversed proposition that, with a movable pulley, the weight capable of being lifted is twice the force applied, minus the friction of the apparatus.

Combinations of pulleys are arranged with several sheaves in one case to form a block to secure this multiplication of power. The upper or fixed block gives the advantage of position, and

Fig. 21. A length of stud chain with a swivel in the middle.

the lower or movable block, by multiplying the travel of the rope as compared with that of the weight, increases the power in proportionate ratio. Briefly, the weight capable of being lifted is equal to the force multiplied by the number of ropes supporting the lower or movable block.

261

Examination of the block and tackle shown in Fig. 23 will make this clear, the arrow heads showing the direction of travel of the rope, or fall as it is termed. The thin cord shown manipulates a patent brake, seen in the upper block, which locks the rope should it be desired to suspend the object lifted. It will be evident, upon consideration, that no two sheaves travel at the same velocity, because of the varying speed of the different parts of the rope. It is therefore necessary that the sheaves be independent of each other, revolving loosely upon a spindle fixed in the shell or frame of the block. A basic factor of all mechanical powers is, that whatever is lost in time is gained in load lifted, or the reverse. It has been seen that with the weight traveling half as fast as the rope, double the weight could be lifted with the same force, or a force of only half the weight was necessary. In practice, the friction losses must be considered in estimating the power required to lift loads by blocks.

Example—What force (pull) must be applied on a block and tackle having four rope lengths shortened to lift 500 lbs.

For four rope lengths (according to Table 2), the ratio of load-to-pull is 3.3. Accordingly, a force applied = 500 ÷ 3.3 = 151.5 lbs.

Example—If a pull of 100 lbs. is applied on a block and tackle having a ratio of load-to-pull of 4.33, what load can be lifted?

100 × 4.33 = 433 lbs.

Table 2. Working Loads of Rope Blocks

Number of Rope Lengths Shortened	Manila Rope		Wire Rope	
	Ratio of Load to Pull	Efficiency, Per Cent	Ratio of Load to Pull	Efficiency, Per Cent
2	1.91	96	....	....
3	2.64	88	2.73	91
4	3.30	83	3.47	87
5	3.84	77	4.11	82
6	4.33	72	4.70	78
7	4.72	67	5.20	74
8	5.08	64	5.68	71
9	5.37	60	6.08	68
10	....	....	6.46	65
12	....	....	7.08	59

Figure 22. A common
anchor shackle.

DIFFERENTIAL BLOCKS

The heavy-duty type of hoist or chain block was invented by Thomas A. Weston in 1854, and is comparatively inexpensive and simple in construction. It is based upon the principle of the Chinese windlass shown in Fig. 24. An inspection will show that the differential block depends upon a very slow speed of the weight in comparison with the speed of the haul. This is secured by making the two upper drums nearly the same size, the endless chain being paid out by one while it is hove in by the other. In other words, the smaller drum tends to lower the weight while the larger one raises it, the total lift equalling the difference of circumference of the two drums.

WORM HOIST

In this type of hoist (sometimes called screw hoist), the power is transmitted from a hand chain to the load chain by worm gearing, the principle of transmission being shown in Fig. 25.

In the worm hoist, an endless chain passes around a sprocket wheel and rotates a worm, and by multiplying gearing, hauls on the lifting chain. Not only is the gain of power at the expense of time obtained by the multiple gearing of this device, but the worm prevents slipping and, as there is no weight on the hand chain, a jam is not dangerous.

SPUR GEAR AND DRUM HOIST

This type of hoist is known as a winch which, by definition, is a

263

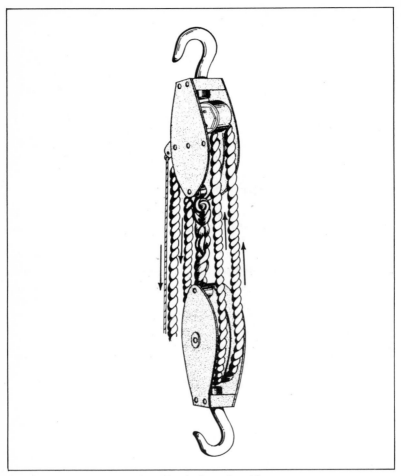

Fig. 23. Block and tackle.

windlass, particularly one used for hoisting, as on a truck or the mast of a derrick. A winch usually has one or more hand cranks geared to a drum around which the rope or chain pulls a load. Fig. 26 shows a simple winch with single reduction gearing. It is equipped with a brake for lowering and controlling operations.

264

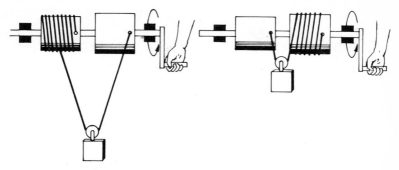

Fig. 24. The Chinese windlass illustrating the principle of the differential hoist.

When using a winch of this description with wire rope, the barrel or drum should be at least twenty times the diameter of the rope.

THE SUPPORTING STRUCTURE

Erectors will find the *gin pole* of great use; this is a stout pole, of a suitable length, which serves as a portable derrick. The gin pole and the method of using it in placing a mast in position is shown in Fig. 27.

The *tripod or shear legs* is an old and well-known hoisting device, and is shown in Fig. 28. It consists of three sticks or legs fastened together at the top and from this point the tackle is suspended. Different methods of fastening the legs together are used.

Another form of supporting structure consisting of a mast of suitable height and fixed by braces on a triangular base, is shown in Fig. 29. The term *stiff leg* is applied to distinguish this mast from the mast secured by guy cables, as in Fig. 27.

By definition, a *derrick* is an apparatus for lifting and moving heavy weights. It is similar to the crane, but differs from it by having a boom. The boom corresponds to the jib of the crane, and is pivoted at the lower end so that it may take different inclinations from the perpendicular. The weight is suspended from the end of the boom by ropes or chains that pass through a block at the end of the boom, and directly to the crab, or winding apparatus at the foot of the post. Another rope connects the top of the boom

265

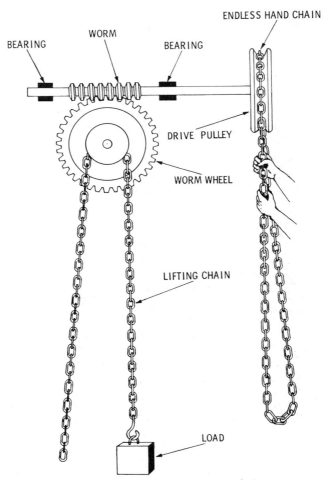

BEARING

WORM

BEARING

ENDLESS HAND CHAIN

DRIVE PULLEY

WORM WHEEL

LIFTING CHAIN

LOAD

Fig. 25. Elementary worm gear hoist.

with a block at the top of the post, and then passes to the motor
below.

The motions of the derrick are:

1. A direct lift.
2. A circular motion around the axis of the post.

Fig. 26. Crab or hand winch.

3. A radial motion within the circle described by the point of the boom.

The *pile driver* is equipped with a very substantial supporting structure and, while not a hoisting rig in the general sense of the term, its operation depends upon hoisting a heavy weight.

SUMMARY

A hoist is a machine for raising or lowering heavy or bulky items. Some form of hoist is generally necessary in the construction of a building, as for instance in placing heavy girders or beams, sections of wall frames, roof trusses, etc. A means must be provided for attaching the load, proper reduction of gears, and proper size hoist for the work load.

Various types of ropes are used in hoist operation. Generally, the most popular rope used is three- and four-strand manila. The

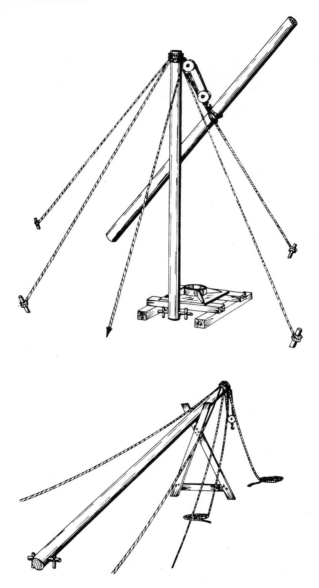

Fig. 27. Gin pole.

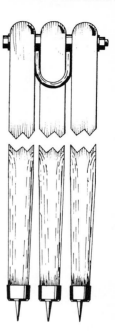

Fig. 28. Tripod or shear legs.

four-strand is stronger and has an even surface. It also weighs more per foot and is constructed around a center core, which keeps the strands away from the center, thus reducing chafing as the rope is bent around the pulley.

Care of rope is important, and constant inspection is necessary. A good method of inspecting the inside fibers is by partially untwisting the strands to inspect the core and inside portion of each strand. Rope that has been used in the rain or allowed to get into water should be hung up to dry. Hemp will easily rot if gotten wet.

Passing a rope over a fixed pulley for hoisting a weight does not give any increase in power. A combination of ropes and pulleys used to gain a mechanical advantage in lifting a load is known as a block and tackle. In the worm hoist, an endless chain

269

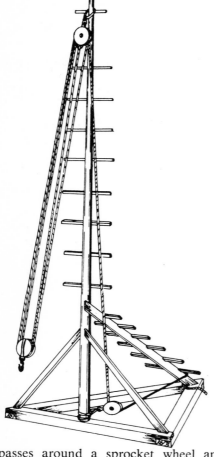

Fig. 29. Stiff-leg mast.

passes around a sprocket wheel and rotates a worm, and by multiple gearing, hauls on the lifting chain.

REVIEW QUESTIONS

1. Why is four-strand rope stronger than three-strand?
2. What are the advantages in using a four-strand rope?
3. What is laying, relaying, and whipping a rope?
4. Explain the operations of a worm-gear hoist.
5. What is a block and tackle?

CHAPTER 17

Rope Splicing

The splice in a transmission rope is not only the weakest part of the rope, but it is the first to fail when the rope is worn out. If the splice is not of sufficient strength, the rope will fail by breakage or pulling out of the splice. If the rope is larger at the splice, the projecting parts will wear out on the sheaves and the rope will fail by cutting off of the strands.

Splicing may be termed as the operation of joining two parts of the same rope or separate ropes, by interweaving the strands so that the resulting joint is about the same size as the original rope.

The splices used by riggers are:

1. The long splice.
2. The short splice.
3. The tapered splice.
4. The eye splice.

The *long splice* is made by unlaying one strand of each rope, replacing it by a strand of the other rope, and then fastening by knots, with the resulting joints no larger than the original rope. In a *short splice,* each strand of each rope is carried over the adjacent strand, and tucked under the second strand, and so on. In the *eye splice,* the end part of the rope is bent into a loop, and then spliced into the standing part with a short splice. The tools required for splicing consist of a pair of nippers for cutting off ends of strands, a wood spike for opening strands, and a wooden mallet to hammer down any uneven surfaces.

271

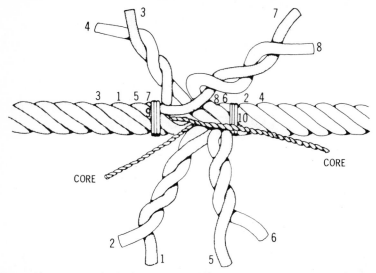

Fig. 1. Showing method of seizing rope prior to actual splicing operation.

How To Make a Long Splice

The procedure to follow when making a long splice in a manila rope is shown in the following illustrations, and is as follows:

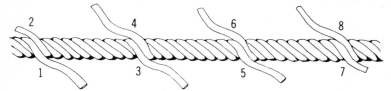

Fig. 2. Showing meeting point of strands.

1. Tie a piece of twine (9 and 10 in Fig. 1) around the rope to be spliced, about six feet from each end. Then unlay the strands of each end back to the twine.
2. Butt the ropes together and twist each corresponding pair of strands loosely to keep them from being tangled, as shown in Fig. 1.
3. Twine 10 is now cut and strand 8 unlaid, with strand 7 carefully laid in its place for a distance of four and one-half feet from the junction.

272

4. Strand 6 is next unlaid about one and one-half feet, with strand 5 laid in its place. The ends of the cores are now cut off so they just meet.

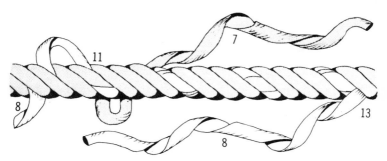

Fig. 3. Illustrating treatment of half strands.

5. Next unlay strand 1 four and one-half feet, laying strand 2 in its place. Unlay strand 3 one and one-half feet, laying in strand 4.

6. Cut all the strands off to a length of about twenty inches, for convenience in the manipulation. The rope now assumes the form shown in Fig. 2, with the meeting points of the strands three feet apart.

From this point, each pair of strands is successfully subjected to the following operation:

7. From their point of meeting, unlay strands 7 and 8 three turns; split both strands 7 and 8 in halves as far back as they are now unlaid, and "whip" the end of each half strand with a small piece of twine.

8. Half of strands 7 and 8 is now laid in three turns. The half strands now meet and are tied in a single knot (11 in Fig. 3), making the rope at this point its original size.

9. The rope is now opened with the wooden spike, and the half strand 7 worked around the half strand of 8 by passing the end of the half strand 7 through the rope, as shown in Fig. 3, and drawn taut. Again work this half strand around until it reaches strand 13, which was not laid in. Strand 13 is now split, and the half strand 7 is drawn through

the opening thus made, and then tucked under the two adjacent stands, as shown in Fig. 4.

10. Next the other half of strand 8 is wound around the other half strand of 7 in the same manner. Finally, after each pair of strands has been treated in this manner, the ends are cut off at 12, leaving them about four inches long. After a few days the cut strands will draw into the body

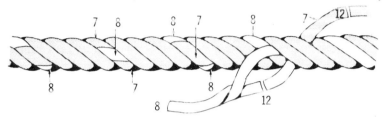

Fig. 4. Showing completed splice prior to cutting of ends.

of the rope or wear off, so that the locality of the splice can barely be detected.

How to Make an Eye Splice

An eye splice, as the name implies, is one in which the end of a rope is spliced in the form of an eye or ring. To make an eye splice, proceed as follows:

1. Unlay the rope for a distance sufficient to make four tucks.
2. Hold the bight in the left hand, and place the unlaid part

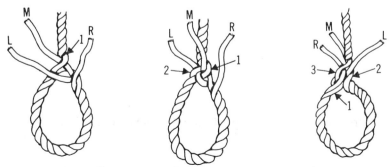

Fig. 5. Illustrating method of making an eye splice.

of the rope over the bight. Hold the middle strand *M* over strand 2 with the thumb and first finger of the left hand.

3. Tuck the middle strand *M* under strand 1, as illustrated in Fig. 5.
4. Next, lay strand *L* over strand 1 and tuck it under strand 2, as shown in Fig. 5.
5. Now turn the splice over and tuck strand *R* under strand 3, as shown in Fig. 5.
6. Continue tucking the strands in the same order as that in the short splice.

How To Make a Grommet

By definition, a grommet is a ring formed by twisting on itself a single strand of an unlaid rope. The size of the ring to be formed depends upon the particular application of the grommet. To make a grommet, proceed as follows:

1. Use a single strand of rope four times as long as the circumference of the finished grommet. Form a circle of the size desired.
2. Lead the long end of the strand around, following the grooves or *lay* of the strand, until a two-strand circle or ring has been formed, as illustrated in Fig. 6.
3. Continue twisting the free end between the turns already made until a three-stranded ring is complete.
4. Tie the ends with a overhand knot.
5. Pass the remaining ends under the nearest strand, and trim closely.

If a strong twist is kept on the strand while laying up the grommet, the finished ring will be as smooth as a finished rope, as shown in Fig. 6.

WIRE ROPES AND SPLICING METHOD

Wire ropes are built up of strands made of wires twisted together, the numbers of wires commonly used being four, seven, twelve, nineteen, and thirty-seven. Ordinarily, the wires are twisted into strands in the opposite direction to the twist of the strands in the finished rope.

275

Fig. 6. Method of making a grommet.

When the wires and strands are twisted in the same direction, the rope is known as *long lay* rope, and when in the opposite direction it is known as a *regular lay* rope. The standard wire rope consists of six strands twisted around a hemp center. A wire strand is sometimes used instead of a hemp center. This adds to the strength of the rope but causes it to wear more rapidly.

Factors of Safety

The breaking strength of wire ropes seldom exceeds 90% of the aggregate strength of all the wires, the average being about 80%. It is never advisable for the working load of a wire rope used for general purposes, particularly running ropes, to exceed one-fifth of the breaking strength. This means that the safety factor should not be less than five.

To determine the proper working load, divide the breaking strength by the proper safety factor. For example, a wire rope having a breaking strength of 10,000 lbs. with a safety factor of five, the proper working load would be 2,000 lbs. Safety factors in excess of five (varying up to eight and even more), are required for safe and economical operation. The proper safety factor for a wire rope should be determined by careful and thorough consideration of all pertinent data. Such data should include all loads, acceleration, deceleration, rope speed, and rope attachments; the number, size, and arrangement of all sheaves and drums; existing conditions causing corrosion and abrasion; length of rope required; economical rope life, and degree of danger to life and property.

No fixed arbitrary values for the safety factor can be properly set for the various classifications of service. These can safely vary,

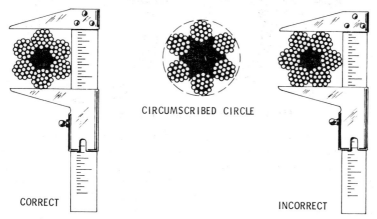

CIRCUMSCRIBED CIRCLE

CORRECT   INCORRECT

Fig. 7. Illustrating the correct and incorrect method of measuring wire rope diameter.

within limits, with the conditions present on individual installations, and should any doubt arise, the manufacturer of the equipment should be consulted.

Wire Rope Measurement

The correct measurement of a wire rope is that of the circumscribed circle. Stated differently, the correct measurement is that of a true circle enclosing the rope. Therefore, care should be taken when measuring to obtain this diameter in the manner shown in Fig. 7.

WIRE ROPE SPLICING

The tools required for wire rope splicing are shown in Fig. 8, and consist of the following:

1. Two "T" shaped splicing pins.
2. Two round splicing pins.
3. A tapered spike for removing strands and fiber core.
4. A knife for cutting the fiber core.
5. A pair of wire cutters for cutting off ends of the strands.

277

6. Two wooden mallets to hammer down any uneven surface.
7. A piece of fiber rope spliced endless.
8. A hickory stick the size of an ordinary hammer handle, which is used to untwist the strands.

There are four types of splices generally used for wire rope:

1. Standard splice.
2. Chicago or tied splice.
3. Splice for ropes with an independent wire rope core.
4. Thimble splice.

General Splicing Practice

The making of rope splices in the field is usually performed by men who possess a certain amount of mechanical skill and a facility in handling tools. It would therefore be well for those who are entirely lacking in experience to make several practice splices prior to attempting to splice a rope which will be subjected to severe conditions in actual use. If the first effort to produce a satisfactory result fails, a review of the work will reveal where the mistake was made, and will indicate what must be avoided in the future. It is extremely important in making a splice to use great care in laying the various rope strands firmly into position. If, during any of the various operations, some of the strands are not pulled tightly into their respective places in the finished splice, it is doubtful that satisfactory results will be obtained.

When such a poorly made splice is put into service, the strands which are relatively slack will not receive their full share of the load, thus causing the remaining strands to be excessively stressed. The unbalanced condition will result in a distorted relative position of the rope strands, so that some of these will project above the surface of the rope and be subjected to excessive abrasion and abuse. It is strongly recommended that during each of the splicing steps, particular attention be paid to maintaining, as nearly as possible, the same degree of tightness in all of the strands in the splice. When ropes are to be used in places where failure would endanger human life, the splicing should be done only by men who are experienced in such work. It is a good practice to test such splices to at least twice their maximum working load before placing them in service.

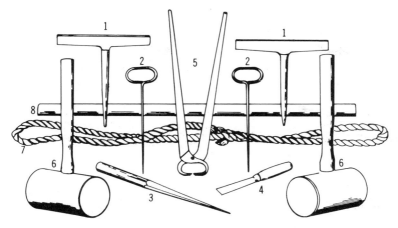

Fig. 8. Typical wire rope splicing tools.

Seizing Operation

Before cutting a wire rope for splicing, it is essential to place at least three sets of seizings on each side of the intended cut to prevent disturbing the uniformity of the rope. On large diameter ropes, more seizings are necessary and, unless a serving mallet is used, each standard seizing should consist of eight snug and close-wound wraps of seizing wire. The clearance between seizings should be about one rope diameter.

SUMMARY

Splicing a rope not only makes it the weakest part, but it is the first to fail when the rope is worn out. If the splice is not strong enough, it will fail by breaking or by pulling out of the splice. If the splice is too large in diameter, it will wear out on the pulley by cutting the strands.

A splice may be defined as joining two parts of the same rope, or separate rope, by interweaving the strands so that the joint is about the same diameter as the original rope. Various splices are

279

used, such as the long, short, eye, and tapered splice. The tools required for splicing consist of a pair of nippers for cutting the ends of the rope, a wood spike to open the rope strands, and a wooden mallet to hammer down any uneven surfaces.

Wire rope is built up of strands made of wires twisted together. The number of wires generally used is four, seven, twelve, nineteen, and thirty-seven. Ordinarily, the wires are twisted into strands in the opposite direction to the twist of the strands in a finished rope. When wires or strands are all twisted in the same direction, the rope is known as long lay. When they are twisted in the opposite direction, it is known as a regular lay rope.

REVIEW QUESTIONS

1. Name the various splices used by riggers.
2. What is the difference between long lay rope and regular lay rope?
3. What are the four standard splices used for wire rope?
4. Why is it a good idea to practice rope splicing before actual repair is done?
5. What is the correct method used in measuring wire rope diameter?

Useful Information

To find the circumference of a circle, multiply the diameter by 3.1416.

To find the diameter of a circle, multiply the circumference by .31831.

To find the area of a circle, multiply the square of the diameter by .7854.

The radius of a circle $\times$ 6.283185 = the circumference.

The square of the circumference of a circle $\times$ .07958 = the area.

Half the circumference of a circle $\times$ half its diameter = the area.

The circumference of a circle $\times$ .159155 = the radius.

The square root of the area of a circle $\times$ .56419 = the radius.

The square root of the area of a circle $\times$ 1.12838 = the diameter.

To find the diameter of a circle equal in area to a given square, multiply a side of the square by 1.12838.

To find the side of a square equal in area to a given circle, multiply the diameter by .8862.

To find the side of a square inscribed in a circle, multiply the diameter of the circle by .7071.

To find the side of a hexagon inscribed in a circle, multiply the diameter of the circle by .500.

To find the diameter of a circle inscribed in a hexagon, multiply a side of the hexagon by 1.7321.

To find the side of an equilateral triangle inscribed in a circle multiply the diameter of the circle by .866.

To find the diameter of a circle inscribed in an equilateral triangle, multiply a side of the triangle by .57735.

To find the area of the surface of a ball (sphere), multiply the square of the diameter by 3.1416.

To find the volume of a ball (sphere), multiply the cube of the diameter by .5236.

Doubling the diameter of a pipe increases its capacity four times.

To find the pressure in pounds per square inch at the base of a column of water, multiply the height of the column in feet by .433.

A gallon of water (U.S. Standard) weighs 8.336 pounds and contains 231 cubic inches. A cubic foot of water contains 7 1/2 gallons, 1728 cubic inches, and weighs 62.425 pounds at a temperature of about 39°F.

NOTES

NOTES

NOTES

Index